DEFINING IT SUCCESS THROUGH THE SERVICE CATALOG

Other publications by Van Haren Publishing on IT Management

Van Haren Publishing specializes in titles on Best Practices, methods and standards within IT and business management. These publications are grouped in two series: ITSM Library (on behalf of ITSMF Netherlands) and Best Practice. Current and forthcoming titles include:

ITIL ®:
- Foundations of IT Service Management based on ITIL, (English, Dutch, French, German, Japanese, Chinese, Danish, Russian, Spanish, Italian; Korean and Arabic editions due Autumn 2006; also available as a CD-ROM)
- IT Service Management based on ITIL (German, French, Japanese, Russian, Spanish, Danish)
- IT Service Management - een samenvatting, 2de druk, A Pocket Guide (Dutch)
- IT Service Management - een leerboek (Dutch)

ISO/IEC 20000:
- ISO/IEC 20000 - A Pocket Guide (English) ISO 27001 and ISO 17799:
- Information Security based on ISO 27001 and ISO 17799 - A Management Guide (English)
- Implementing Information Security based on ISO 27001 and ISO 17799 - A Management Guide (English)

CobiT:
- IT Governance based on CobiT - A Pocket Guide (English, German)

IT Service CMM:
- IT Service CMM - A Pocket Guide (English)

ASL:
- ASL - A Framework for Application Management (English)
- ASL - Application Services Library - A Management Guide (English, Dutch)

BiSL:
- BiSL - A Framework for Business Management and Information Management (Dutch; English edition due Autumn 2006)
- BiSL - Business information Services Library - A Management Guide (Dutch; English edition due Autumn 2006)

ISPL:
- IT Services Procurement op basis van ISPL (Dutch)
- IT Services Procurement based on ISPL - A Pocket Guide (English)

PRINCE2™:
- Project Management based on PRINCE2™- Edition 2005 (Dutch, English, German)

MSP:
- Programme Management based on MSP (Dutch, English)
- Programme Management based on MSP - A Management Guide (English)

MoR:
- Risk Management based on MoR - A Management Guide (English)

Topics & Management instruments:
- Metrics for IT Service Management (English)
- Six Sigma for IT Management (English)

MOF/MSF:
- MOF - Microsoft Operations Framework, A Pocket Guide (Dutch, English, French, German, Japanese)
- MSF - Microsoft Solutions Framework, A Pocket Guide (English, German)

For the latest information on VHP publications, visit our website: www.vanharen.net

Defining
IT Success through
the Service Catalog

A practical guide about the positioning, design and
deployment of an actionable catalog of IT Services

Colophon

Title:	Defining IT Success through the Service Catalog
Authors:	Troy Du Moulin - Pink Elephant Rodrigo Flores and Bill Fine - newScale
Editor:	Inform-IT, Groningen -- NL
Publisher:	Van Haren Publishing, Zaltbommel, www.vanharen.net
ISBN (10):	90 77212 96 5
ISBN (13):	978 90 77212 96 7
Print:	First edition, first impression, January 2007
Layout and design:	CO2 Premedia, Amersfoort -- NL
Copyright:	Pink Elephant Inc. and newScale Inc. 2007

For any further enquiries about Van Haren Publishing, please send an email to: info@vanharen.net

Table of Contents

Acknowledgements

I dedicate this book to my fellow Pinkers and my network of close friends and associates in the IT Service Management arena. This book would not have happened without long conversations and healthy debate.

To my wife Christine and three sons Caleb, Noah and Jordan, I thank you for the time you have allowed me to be on the road about the business of business transformation and have put up with the challenges of balancing work and family life over the last few years.
Troy

We thank all newScalers that have brought passion, dedication and a wonderful can-do attitude in helping our customers realize their goals. We also dedicate this to our many, many customers who have challenged and trusted us to partner alongside them.

Finally, we dedicate this book to the Flores family - all three generations - who helped give birth to this adventure. And specially, to our wives who put up with strange hours, dark mutterings, assorted absences and too much techno music while we wrote this book.
Rodrigo and Bill

Preface

The subject of IT and business alignment is a popular one. While not to downplay this topic's importance, one needs to ask *why* it is so popular. Concerns about HR and business alignment, or finance and business alignment are not prominent. The very fact that IT and business alignment are relevant topics today tells us something about the level of maturity of our industry.

Most IT organizations around the world are at the very early stages of an evolution – transforming from technology-focused organizations to service-focused organizations. The challenge is how to convince both the 'techies' and the business customers that IT does not simply manage hardware and software.

As the evolution to a Service Delivery model continues, it is important to understand where the industry came from and how Technology Management differs in focus from Service Management. Over the last 20 years IT planning, strategy, recruitment, skills training, and reward and incentive programs focused on developing centers of technology excellence. Individuals were hired, and trained to hone their technology skills in order to optimize and reduce cost around the use of new technology innovation. However, for the most part education about the business perspective was largely ignored. Nowhere is this clearer than the fact that most computer science degrees have, until recently, been purely technology-focused with little or no focus on teaching general business principles.

The service mentality evolution starts with the awareness that a customer facing service cannot be understood as collections of like technology, segregated by domain, platform, or protocol. And that it is the rudimentary responsibility of IT to understand how any given IT component enables or disables a business process. Until this is known it is difficult to claim that IT is aligned to business goals.

The IT world has become more networked, the software stacks have acquired more layers of abstraction (application servers, database, web servers, business intelligence, etc), and devices have proliferated (mobility is going to double the number of devices per employee). As a result it is easy to lose the relationship between an IT Service and its business value. The IT Service does not live in a machine or a software package. It is distributed across hundreds of devices and software components.

While we are not futurists, we can safely predict this: there will be more data, more devices, more software, new stacks and new dependencies. As organizations become more networked and concepts like WIKIs, blogging and web 2.0 mashups are adopted, it will be harder and harder to figure out where an IT Service starts and ends and, consequently, more difficult to describe, measure, cost and govern these services.

The purpose of this book is to help the reader develop practices and disciplines for IT Service Design and Governance. IT Service Design, at its core, is the ability to communicate what IT does in a manner that enables the business to demand and consume IT resources appropriately and responsibly, and in line with business priorities. IT Service Governance relates to the actual design and specification of a service and its structure with sufficient rigor that IT operations can build it, run it and manage it. Bringing IT Service Design and Governance together is, we believe, the next evolutionary step for IT.

About Pink Elephant

Pink Elephant is the world leader in IT management best practices, offering solutions to public and private businesses globally, and many listed in the Fortune 500. The Company specializes in improving the quality of IT services through the application of recognized frameworks, including the Information Technology Infrastructure Library (ITIL). For more information, please visit www.pinkelephant.com.

1

Why Service Catalogs?

Technology commoditization is driving changes and new priorities for IT organizations. Moore's law[1], open source and global sourcing have all made technology widely available, standardized and cheaper than ever. Business management is responding with an ever-increasing willingness to outsource key IT functions and entire IT departments.

In this context, does IT matter? This is the question author Nicholas Carr asked in his book of the same title, and a sea change in attitude was unleashed on the shores of an unsuspecting IT organization. Carr's basic argument is that IT Services are becoming increasingly commoditized, and as such, provide little opportunity for competitive advantage to the business. If everyone has the same capability, then IT is not a differentiator, but rather a risk that needs to be managed and a cost that needs to be controlled. How much market differentiation is email delivering to your organization? The answer is none.

The result is a cost-dominated conversation between IT and the business, where IT is facing increasing pressure to account for and reduce cost wherever possible. The old axiom of 'doing more with less' has never had such an impact on IT operations and support as it does today. Thousands of IT Managers are being placed in a situation which compels them to defend their staffing levels against both internal and external threats.

To address this situation, IT Executives are being forced to gain a better understanding of the services they provide, and undertake an accurate cost-benefit analysis of why these services are better value than services being offered by managed service providers who promise fixed or known costs.

As is the case with any business, IT is asked to develop a catalog that defines the scope, characteristics and costs of available services and products, and allows for better management of the IT environment as a whole. The basic requirement to do all this is to have a clear

---

1　Moore's Law refers to the concept of technology's growing complexity and functionality coupled with the ever shrinking size of the technology.

definition of the services the IT organization provides, the components and resources that make up the service, and the associated costs for these services.

The sad fact of the matter is that very few IT organizations have developed a Service Catalog that articulates what they do and what they offer at this level of detail. The opportunity, however, is that organizations embracing this challenge have the ability to become more than just a commodity supplier. The role of IT in the future, we believe, demands that both IT organizations and managed service providers evolve beyond technological competence and effective cost-management, to a role in which they enable the management of business risk and alignment of IT investments with business value. The cornerstone of this evolution is the IT Service Catalog.

■ 1.1 Beyond Cost Center - managing business risk

While in recent years the primary focus of IT has been the cost-optimization of technology domains, applications and components, the growing interest in service management represents a revolution occurring within the IT industry. This revolution is fueled by a growing understanding that there is no real separation between technology and business process. Business finance provides a good example. When it is understood that a financial process like accounts payable or accounts receivable cannot truly be separated from its underlying application system then it is also understood that not only does IT facilitate innovation, but it also represents business risk. In essence Information Technology can no longer be seen simply as a cost somehow separate and distinct from the processes it automates. It has gone from being an option to a necessity, from an innovation to a utility.

This fact is magnified by regulations now in place, such as Sarbanes-Oxley, HIPAA, Basel II and a myriad of others, that affect how IT is expected to control and manage risks. This is a permanent change in the role of IT. Business leaders are now keenly aware of the impact their IT infrastructure can have on their careers and personal freedom. They have awoken to the co-dependence of modern business on IT.

Catalogs as a means to effective governance

The IT industry as a whole is undergoing a transformation from an industry largely shaped by the leadership and personalities of individual IT executives and vendors, to one that is becoming more defined, homogeneous and regulated. Until recently, each organization's IT functions, controls and processes were largely defined by the company culture and the personalities of a series of Chief Information Officers (CIOs) and technical heroes. Based on this observation, it is not surprising to find the practices and definitions of IT Governance are vastly different from organization to organization.

The recent formalization of the concept, scope and role of IT Governance is largely being driven by a series of legislative initiatives emerging around the world relating to Enterprise or Business Governance. These legislations focus on the duties of public and private companies to act in a manner of trust in relationship to the maintenance and security of customer data and the publishing of accurate financial information. This change in view is based on the understanding that core business transactions and data are directly linked to the IT Services and systems which store and publish this information, as well as the IT structures and processes which control and support these systems. As a result, governments around the world are requiring that IT organizations become accountable, formalized and auditable for their IT practices, processes and controls.

To achieve this objective, a global movement is evolving to formalize the scope of IT Governance as a consistent model, regardless of industry sector and geographic location. In short, IT is moving away from a model of informal and ad-hoc controls towards a regulated model of codes and practices. The concept of regulatory code is not new. Consider building and electrical codes that are designed to protect people and businesses. Many industry analysts espouse the concept of utility computing; the logical next step is to apply a code of practice to this new utility. In short, IT Governance is primarily concerned with supporting the objectives of Enterprise Governance and in doing so, establishes the basis for sound and aligned provisioning of services to the Business Customer. The ultimate driver for good governance should be related to meeting business goals and complying with regulatory and risk management issues facing Enterprise Governance.

The role of Service Level Management (SLM) and its primary tool, the Service Catalog, are critical success factors in the process of moving to repeatable and auditable service provision. The Service Catalog represents a trusted record of the services provided by IT, its default capabilities, measures and primary means of access and provision. In short the Service Catalog represents the value IT provides to business enablement:
- What is not defined cannot be controlled;
- What is not controlled and stabilized cannot be measured;
- What is not measured consistently cannot be improved.

IT Governance definition
According to the IT Governance Institute (ITGI):

"IT Governance is the responsibility of the board of directors and executive management. It is an integral part of Enterprise Governance and consists of the leadership, organizational structures and processes that ensure that the organization's IT sustains and extends the organization's strategies and objectives." (Source: Board Briefing on IT Governance, IT Governance Institute, 2003)

The scope of responsibility of IT Governance has been summarized by the ITGI as covering the following areas:
- Strategic Alignment: With focus on aligning IT strategy and planning.
- Value Delivery: Optimizing service delivery, processes, quality and speed with expense.
- Risk Management: Addressing and ensuring the safe guarding of IT assets.

- Resource Management: Optimizing knowledge, IT environments, structures and establishing accountability.
- Performance Management: Monitoring IT Services and tracking project delivery.

These high-level objectives are also in line with SLM's process objectives and the development of an IT Service Catalog.

The interest in IT Service Management, the passage of business legislation that impacts IT (such as the Sarbanes-Oxley Act of 2002, or SOX), and the interest in standards are symptomatic of something fundamental to these governance principles. At the root of this focus on service, process and legislation is a growing awareness that there is no separation between business processes and the underlying IT Services and systems.

IT has become so vital to business that companies literally cannot function without it. For several years, organizations have increasingly leveraged IT to optimize the cost and efficiency of business processes. It's clear that no one is likely to revert to manual processes. Ultimately this means that every business process - whether it is banking, energy production, product shipping, invoicing, or something else - is dependent on business applications and infrastructure services. If the way a specific critical IT component enables or disables a business process is not understood, then the IT function cannot truly claim to be aligned with business. The process of understanding how IT relates to business starts with the definition and design of business-focused IT Services, which in turn is represented in an integrated Service Catalog.

Catalogs and ITIL®
The IT Infrastructure Library (ITIL) framework was among the first to advocate that IT organizations begin process improvement initiatives by defining and documenting a portfolio of standard service offerings in a Service Catalog. ITIL recommends the development of a Service Catalog as the first step in the SLM process. The most recent ITIL Business Perspective publication reinforces the need to use a Service Catalog as the focal point for interactions between IT and business unit executives.

ITIL defines the Service Catalog as a list of services that should be presented in business terms. However, it does not provide concrete guidance about how to build a Service Catalog or recommendations about how best to make the catalog actionable and operational. In theory, the advice is sound – in practice, it has been difficult for many IT organizations to implement it. Too often, following this guidance leads to a significant investment of time to create numerous documents in an effort to develop a static Service Catalog that no customer will ever read or act upon. The primary purpose of this book is to help fill this void, and provide guidance to the practitioner.

■ 1.2 Beyond Cost Center - managing business value

Once IT evolves from the management of technology, to the management of cost and business risk, the next step is to manage the alignment of the investment in IT capabilities with business value. The growing interest in service management is not only based on risk, but also on the desire to improve the quality, delivery, and value-add of IT Services. Done well, the development of Service Catalogs and Service Level Agreements (SLAs) can define success for IT operations and service delivery in alignment with the needs of the business.

The central challenge, however, is that the average IT organization today cannot articulate business value and cannot describe service quality in customer language. IT talks storage, the business talks stores; IT talks servers, the customer talks services. There's no visibility on what IT does or its cost structure. There are multiple channels to get anything done and most of them are broken. The business has no way to meaningfully compare against external service providers.

Compare this situation to other areas of the business and IT seems less than professional. A manufacturing manager sits in front of the IT director and says, "I can give you the run-down of my costs down to the cellophane wrapper, and I use that information to drive efficiencies in my supply chain. I want the same kind of detailed information from IT so I can drive those costs down." And many want market-based standardization so they can compare costs and efficiencies with other providers.

It's not that IT leaders don't get it, but they find it difficult to innovate when 70-90% of budget is already committed to keeping the lights on. There's clearly a disconnect between the demands and expectations of capability of the business and what IT can actually supply. The disconnect between business goals and IT priorities consistently ranks among the top three issues facing CIOs year after year. While the specific wording varies from survey to survey, the strong message is the same – business unit executives and End Users alike don't trust that IT is working on the right things to move the business forward.

The trust deficit
Lack of trust creates a no-win cycle for the IT organization and the business as a whole. The cycle often starts when End Users' expectations for some of the basic services offered by IT are not met – a new PC is delivered later than expected, or setting up a new email account takes the user four phone calls to different help desks.

When the Business Unit asks "What's going on?", IT gets defensive and responds with five-nines up-time percentage charts and acronym-laden language that mean little to anyone outside of IT. At this point, the downward cycle has already begun and trust begins to break. There is no question that up-time is critical, but by itself that does not constitute a service to the customer. This kind of disconnect was well documented by the internal customer of a Fortune 500 IT organization. The customer put together a presentation to kick off an SLA review meeting, which included a slide of a dead animal. It was in response to presentations by IT of its great service level metrics. The slide said: "Yet the animal's still dead." The meaning was, of course, that "your numbers don't mean a thing to my issues".

At the heart of the problem is a breakdown in communication that impacts on trust from multiple directions:
- IT communicates using terminology and context that is difficult for business unit executives and End Users to understand;
- Business unit executives don't understand or have the patience to navigate IT's siloed operations to get the services and innovation needed;
- End Users don't know what to expect from IT, so they set their own expectations.

IT is no longer a monopoly provider, it has hungry and competent competitors after its business. Business unit executives may conclude that IT does not understand – or worse yet, does not care – what they need to run the business. When the time comes to make budgeting and investment decisions, business units are reticent to invest more in their IT black box. They now have options.

The result is that IT budgets either fail to grow as rapidly as the business or, in many cases, shrink compared to previous years. Since more than 70% of IT budgets are typically dedicated to 'keeping the lights on', the remaining 30% allocated for new projects often takes the brunt of these reductions. This means that new projects are often the first to be cut – the same projects that the business counts on for innovation and competitive advantage. Business units' remaining trust that IT is working on the right things vanishes.

Escaping the cycle of distrust

Re-establishing trust between the business and IT means that IT must fundamentally change the way it views its relationship with business units and End Users. A critical first step is a fundamental shift in the mind-set of the IT Service delivery organization. Service delivery is no longer an employee-to-employee, or peer-to-peer relationship. What is needed is a shift to a provider-to-customer relationship where IT continually markets the value of the services offered – where Business Unit executive and End User expectations are not only correctly set, but consistently met.

Today's IT Organizations	Tomorrow's IT Organizations
Focused on Technology	Focused on the Customer
Firefighting Mode	Demand Driven
Organizational 'Stovepipes'	End-to-End Process
Unknown Costs	Financial Transparency
Technical Metrics	Business Value

Table 1.1 IT's role in the enterprise is changing

IT must evolve to become an IT Service provider rather than a technology provider and custodian focused on keeping technology operational by deploying specialists at any cost and on a best-effort results basis. As a service provider, IT focuses on the customer and the services they are actually demanding; it manages the processes from demand to supply to vendor coordination. The decisions about which services to offer and which to outsource is be done in the language of the business, which is financial, rather than technical. Table 1.1 outlines some of the major changes that will occur.

Gone are the days when the internal IT organization owned a monopoly on service delivery. Now, the business demands transparency and visibility into the services and value delivered by IT. Today's Business Unit executives treat IT operations like any other vendor – poorly executed service today means they may shift to another vendor tomorrow. They expect IT to act like a business and be a partner. They expect IT to provide them with a clear catalog of services and effective SLM practices and processes.

How to fail at SLM with SLAs

Many organizations that attempt to improve service fail miserably by starting in the wrong area. Instead of beginning their efforts with the construction of the service offers making up the catalog, they start the process at the last step – the definition of the SLA. IT practitioners naturally gravitate to what they know best – things like server configurations and availability metrics. This is compounded by the fact that many individuals and organizations are directed by well-meaning but misguided advice to start developing their SLM discipline with SLAs as the very first step toward improving business relationships. We think this is a mistake. Instead of approaching SLM from the technology out (i.e. SLAs), we believe organizations must work from the customer in (i.e. the Service Catalog).

IT organizations must understand that SLM's overall objective is to improve customer expectation and relationship around the delivery of IT Services. Most organizations are attempting to do this very thing when they begin to establish SLAs with their customers. However, they do so with little to no understanding of what the business needs, or is willing to pay for, nor what they can offer and reliably deliver. In addition, to this little or no agreement has been gained within the organization about operational agreements of how to support and deliver services within a siloed organization based on technology domains.

The story unfolds like this: a well-meaning IT professional calls a meeting with his or her Business Customer. This meeting is usually initiated by a demand from senior management to establish SLAs on a project plan stating the need for an SLA. The question then is how to develop a SLA in the absence of defined services. Since what is typically measured and understood within IT organizations are the technology domains, SLAs are documented on such things as applications in isolation or infrastructure components such as a server or set of servers. However, none of these things represent the end-to-end service the customer is consuming.

Given this, let us return to the story. Since the individual calling the meeting wishes to be seen as service-oriented, the conversation starts with typical requirements-gathering questions: "We want to be a value-added partner and want to know what you need of IT so that we can enable your business." The answer, not surprisingly, is: "We need IT Services to be reliable, flexible and free." Translated, this means we want it all, we want it now and we don't want to pay for the privilege!

Unfortunately, at this point the IT professional, wishing to be customer-oriented, agrees and documents the customer's wishes in a SLA. However, there is little to no ability to measure whether or not the services will be delivered in accordance with this agreement. And there is little to no chance of the internal groups within IT agreeing on basic support policies around priority, escalation and notification.

The end result of this situation is the creation of a document which is unrealistic and has no real bearing on the IT organization's ability to provide services as promised. The final result of which is failure to deliver on the promises made! What was intended to be a document to improve the relationship and manage expectations became simply a large stick to be beaten over the head with.

By starting the process of SLM before understandingwhat IT Services the customer needed and was willing to pay for (and how they could be delivered reliably), the IT professional achieved the absolute opposite of the original goal of improved customer expectations.

■ 1.3 Starting with the IT Service Catalog

One size does not fit all. That's one of the challenges facing IT organizations that have decided to start with the Service Catalog. The requirements and content are quite different depending on the audience.

The Service Catalog can provide an essential medium for communication and coordination among IT and its customers, and should distinguish between Business Customers (the ones paying for the service) and End Users (the recipients of the service). Satisfying both of these groups is equally important. In either case, the customer is central. To re-establish trust, the IT organization must address the unique needs of both customer segments. Depending on the type of customer, they require a very different view into the Service Catalog.

Service Level Managers, in turn, are responsible for the successful and reliable delivery of Services described within the Service Catalog. A Service Level Manager must be concerned with details that the various customer stakeholders don't need nor want to know. The Service Level Manager requires a detailed view of services and their components, sufficient to understand the relationships, dependencies and underpinning contracts and costs that make up a Service.

The Service Level Manager view

ITIL suggests that the first step in implementing SLM is the development of a comprehensive Service Catalog where services are defined and documented in relationship to their true ability of being delivered with a reasonable level of consistency. Additionally, internal Operational Level Agreements and external Underpinning Contracts need to be established and documented before IT can go to the business to establish agreements around service delivery.

This detail provides the context, attributes and characteristics of how a service will be delivered. Once these foundational elements are in place, the IT organization is in a position to engage the customer in discussions about requirements based on the proven and documented services found within the Service Catalog. It is based on this detail that the Service Level Manager or Account Manager negotiates agreements, establishes costs and defines what metrics are required to evaluate the delivery of IT Services.

Each Service can contain key components documenting attributes of what, how, when and where services can be expected to be delivered. See for example table 1.2.

Description components	Delivery components	Agreement components
• Name of the service	• Service hours	• Identification parties (support, usage)
• Objective of the service • Ownership	• Availability • Level of support	• Requests/amendments/ cancellations • Service reviews
• Target audience • Reporting • Functionality • Configuration • etc.	• Contingency • Performance • Security • etc.	etc.

Table 1.2 Description, delivery and agreement components

As per best practice, the Service Catalog is where the default detail for the services is documented and published. The SLA becomes either a subscription to the default or standard service as documented in the catalog or the documentation of a deviation from the standard offering.

The customer views

Beyond the needs of the Service Level Manager, an effective Service Catalog targets two classes of customer:
• The **executive-level, service portfolio view** of the Service Catalog used by Business Unit executives to understand how IT's portfolio of service offerings map to Business Unit needs. This is sometimes referred to as the 'Service Portfolio' because of its use as a financial budgeting, planning and investment tool.

- The **employee-centric, request-oriented view** of the Service Catalog that is used by End Users (and even other IT staff members) to browse and submit requests for IT Services. This is sometimes referred to as the 'Service Request' or demand catalog because it's used mostly for ordering services.

Individually, either of these views of the Service Catalog can help to re-establish trust. When the two types of Service Catalogs are used in concert as part of a complete Service Portfolio Management solution, IT organizations find they are able to quickly transform the IT-business relationship.

The Business Unit view

Business unit executives need to understand the value that IT delivers. As the economic customer of IT Services, they look for a portfolio view of the service offerings that IT provides at the budget-planning level.

An executive-level service portfolio should describe the broad categories of services, and the fixed and variable cost-drivers, at the same aggregate level that the business units create their budgets. Examples of services represented in a service portfolio include:

- Call Center Operations Hosting: An ERP system to support 2,500 call center users with peak demands of 1,000 orders per hour, support for interfaces to a new order-entry system, and expected turnover of 150 call center staff per month. It includes all required infrastructure services such as bandwidth to call center, disaster recovery planning and 30 report changes per month. Cost drivers could be by person, per received call or per transaction processed.
- Field Repair Service: Enable 300 field-based maintenance and repair staff to access corporate systems from home offices including security, bandwidth and 24x7 Help Desk support. Includes all required infrastructure services such as SOX policy compliance audits, change management processes and asset tracking. The cost is per field staff or per customer visit.
- Retail Store Systems: Opening of 30 new storefronts per quarter including all required IT Services such as email accounts for all employees, cash registers, scanners, access to inventory systems, voice mail, remote back-ups and Internet connectivity. Cost is per store or per employee.

The primary purpose of this catalog is to enable the IT Relationship Manager to accomplish six objectives:

1. Communicate the services that are available from IT so they are linked to operations of the relevant business processes in language and metrics that are relevant to that executive's budget.
2. Provide service level options that allow service quality and costs to be dialed up or down, new services to be added, and old services to be retired based on business impact.
3. Enable budgeting for current, fiscal and future fiscal years.
4. Have the services available as elements for building agreements with the business.
5. Have IT report to the business the actual and forecasted consumption of those services to enable the business to govern consumption.

6. Enable IT to more effectively plan demand and supply of services and resources, including vendor negotiations.

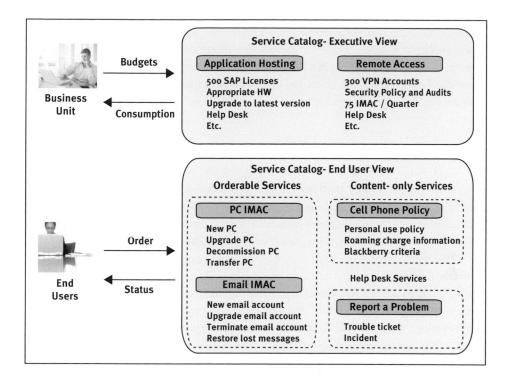

Figure 1.1 Characteristics of different customer views of Service Catalogs

The End User view

End User employees want improved day-to-day service. While business value is important to employees, what's critical is that the day-to-day IT Services they need to perform their job are easily accessible, delivered consistently, and of high quality.

End Users need an actionable and easy-to-use Service Request catalog that describes the services they can order or request from IT. Items in this End User Service Request catalog may include:

- **Orderable services:** Any services where the user initiates a Service Request that results in a series of delivery activities. Examples of orderable services include the traditional IMAC (install, move, add, change) services required to provision a new PC, upgrade an email account or provide access to an application. Other examples include more 'advanced' IT Services – such as application enhancements, or even IT-to-IT requests like setting up a new server to host an application. Delivery plans for orderable services can be fully automated (e.g. access control automatically grants access to a system for a new user), or involve human intervention and delivery (e.g. physically move a server from one location to another).

- **Content-only informational services:** Any services that address a user's informational needs without requiring a delivery activity. Many organizations use content-only informational services to publish and make policy guidelines, who to contact information, FAQs, and other information readily accessible to End Users. Questions may include: "When am I due for a hardware refresh?" and "Who can get a blackberry and why?"
- **Support services:** Support services provide a self-service front end to problem and incident-tracking systems. Users can browse the catalog to find recommended steps to fix common problems – or, in the event this does not work, submit an incident request that generates a traditional trouble ticket in the appropriate Help Desk system.

■   1.4 Putting it all together: the front office of IT

Today most IT organizations are little more than a loose federation of technical and functional silos. IT tends to be defined more in terms of its technical and functional parts (e.g. Desktop, Storage, Service Desk) than as a single, integrated IT organization, much less as an organization that is fully integrated with the business. Going forward IT needs to maintain its ability to deliver within these technical and functional silos, either directly or through external providers. It also needs to put in place the practices, processes and tools to operate effectively as a truly integrated organization, which functions more like a business. The business risks associated with IT Service failure are too great to make infrastructure component changes, for example, without adhering to common, cross-functional Change and Configuration Management processes. Similarly, the services that IT provides its customers are becoming too important and intertwined with the core work of the supported business to leave it up to the customer to assemble the services they may need from the various parts of the IT organization.

If the potential transformation of IT is viewed as "beginning to operate more like a business", the necessity of a Service Catalog becomes apparent. What business today can operate without clearly defining its offers and products in terms its customers will understand and value? A Service Catalog is at the heart of every business large and small. Imagine a restaurant operating without a menu. The menu defines the restaurant and is the means by which the restaurant engages with its customers. Moreover the menu defines the skills required of the cook and the organization of the kitchen, down to the ingredients on the shelf. The same is true of any large multi-national corporation. Every company defines itself in terms of the products and services that its customers consume, and organizes itself to best facilitate the marketing, sales, manufacturing and delivery of those products and services.

The implications for IT organizations are twofold. First, if IT is to truly operate more like a business then it must clearly define a set of offers to its customers, and communicate these to its customers in the form of an IT Service Catalog. The second implication is that the Service Catalog is not a stand-alone concept, but rather is an integral part of the front-office and back-office IT business processes that IT needs to cultivate in order to operate as an integrated business. Much as a Configuration Management Database (CMDB) has value only in the context of the processes it supports (e.g. Change Management, Incident Management, SLM), similarly a Service Catalog must be thought of and created in the context of the key business process it supports. In other words, a successful Service Catalog needs to move beyond the definition of what the IT organization does, to be 'actionable' in the sense that it is an integral part of how services are ordered, delivered, tracked and paid for.

Figure 1.2 identifies at a high level the key, cross-functional processes that modern IT organizations are being asked to put in place to support integrated IT front-office and back-office processes and the relationship of these processes to a Service Catalog.

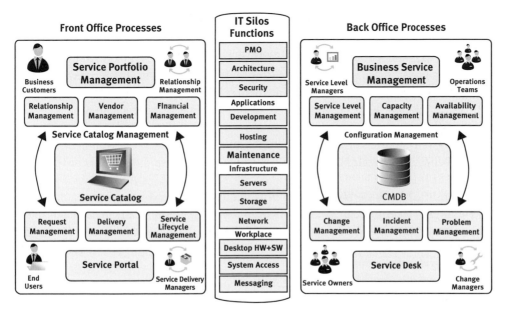

Figure 1.2 Key cross-functional processes

■ 1.5 Looking into the future: an IT maturity model[2]

It is tempting to assume that the ultimate position of IT is to be one of a value driven provider of services to its primary client-'the business'. From these images one gets the mental picture that the business and IT are sitting across the table from each other in a respectful but separate relationship. However, if there is no separation between business processes and information technology, the model of supplier-consumer is again an artificial construct that limits the use and advantage of IT and places both parties at risk.

2　Maturity Model based on writings by Jan Duffy 2002, IT/Business Alignment: Is it an option or is it mandatory?

To put this in perspective, it is important to first understand that Information Technology is only the latest of a series of technological advancements that have pushed business and commerce new levels of automation and efficiency. The introduction of electricity, the advent of transportation systems and the most recent case of manufacturing technology have all gone through a similar model of adoption and integration with business processes. When these earlier technologies were introduced, they were seen as additions to the business models of their day and adopted in increasingly innovative ways until they became so intrinsic to the way business was done that separation was no longer possible. In the early phases of these technology adoptions, specialized management groups were created alongside the business organization to manage and maintain these technologies.

Business planning at the boardroom level for a manufacturing organization would not occur without the inclusion of 'business roles' responsible for assembly line technology. However, this same organization – which is reliant on applications and IT infrastructure to support these older technologies – would not even pause to consider the CIO as an appropriate participant in this planning process. This is because neither the business nor IT has realized that IT is now as much 'the line' as the older and more mature manufacturing technology.

The good news is that this will change as the natural adoption and integration of IT takes place. We believe that as this happens, IT will evolve through four different maturity levels.

Level One: Intuitively connected but practically separated

This first level of maturity represents an organization that philosophically understands that it connects to and supports the business but has no true understanding corporately of how this occurs.

At this level of relationship IT management is focused on the management of component parts and technology domains. The goal of the business organization is to drive down what it believes are uncontrolled costs associated with what it feels is a necessary evil. IT operates in a black box mentality with the business-, "you provide the funds and we will produce the technology". Little or no visibility is provided on how costs are associated with business value.

The siloed approach to managing IT is inefficient. While budgets have remained flat, IT organizations still must support new business initiatives. They face greater pressure to increase efficiency and reduce costs in infrastructure maintenance and IT operations. Different parts of the organization are often unaware of what is happening in other areas and, as a result, groups work at odds with each other. Planning and procurement occur at a departmental level instead of an enterprise level, which leads to IT tools, such as monitoring software, Incident Management systems and inventory products, being purchased redundantly by individual groups.

At this point of maturity, when IT is required to develop SLAs, documents are drawn up against technology components like groups of servers or against an application in isolation to the rest of supporting infrastructure and database elements of the application system.

Without a doubt, the most difficult task facing IT executives at this level of maturity is to convince "techies" that they don't manage boxes and applications in isolation. For example, to the IT organization focused on managing and optimizing technology domains, the processes represented by ITIL, as well as the definition of a Service Catalog, may seem like an incredible overhead or at best a good idea to be done at a later time. This type of organization will not perceive the value of a Service Catalog and will question the benefits. Questions will be raised, such as "Where is the return on investment in implementing these processes and tools?"

Level Two: Are you being served? The supplier-consumer model!

Moving to a service provider model is a significant improvement over a technology management focus. The concept of a customer is well understood and the position of IT as a business enabler is grasped by the IT executive if not by the business executive. At this level there is recognition that IT domains and components cannot be managed in a sense of artificial isolation and there is a project or initiative to understand the relationships and dependency between technology components. It is at this point that a business-focused attempt at developing a Service Catalog is undertaken.

The goal of this organization is to build a best-in-class supplier consumer model where informed discussions around service delivery are supported by a comprehensive catalog of services and documented in customer-facing SLAs.

At this point of the maturity model, internal OLAs have been established to support the service offerings and customer-facing SLAs are inclusive of all of the elements that build the services defined in the catalog. At the earlier stage of maturity the organization struggled with the cost justification of establishing service support and service delivery processes. However, at this level of the model processes such as Incident, Change and SLM are seen as simply the cost of doing business. Logic dictates that to be a service provider, cross-functional processes must be defined and followed by all groups within IT.

However, while this level of maturity represents a significant improvement over the first level, it still propagates the myth that somehow IT is separate and distinct from the business processes. This separation encourages a world view that has the internal IT group perceiving itself to be outside the business walls looking in.

Level Three: Reluctant and awkward dependency

Reluctant dependency refers to a state of maturity where both the business and IT executives realize the interdependency of their organizations. At this point there is a growing realization of risk and ultimate dependency.

It is precisely because of to this understanding of risk and interdependency that governance and legislation have placed requirements on IT controls and processes. The result of this awareness translates into the following scenario:

- The financial results of a company are a direct result of business processes.
- Business processes are dependent on IT Services and systems.
- IT Systems area directly impacted by the maturity and controls of IT processes.
- IT professionals have a direct impact on the consistency of IT processes.

Following this argument there is no true separation between IT and the business. This leads to an interesting discussion when looking at traditional outsourcing sales models focused on outsourcing IT elements believed to be non-core competency. What happens when an organization realizes that IT is at the root of its core competency?

At this stage of maturity, both the IT and business executives struggle with the implications of these conclusions. The positive outcome is that the IT executives now begin to be included at the board table as a peer instead of a service provider.

Level Four: Together we stand, divided we fall

If the first three levels of maturity represent the evolution of an IT organization within the business, the fourth level represents the end state where IT is recognized as an inherent part of the business organization in the same way the preceding technology advancements were. There is now no longer a philosophical organizational separation between IT and the rest of the business. The IT organization is seen, and perceives itself to be, part of the underlying structure that supports the processes represented by the business model.

In a sense the customer is no longer the Business Unit across the table but is now the external customer of the business. Business planning is not attempted without considering current or future technology advancements. Stepping back from this longer term vision of business and IT integration, throughout the balance of this book we will focus on practical next-steps for IT organizations that have recognized both the need for change and the necessity of building from the solid foundation of a robust and effective Service Catalog.

1. We will answer the question of what constitutes a Service. We will talk in both general terms about the notion of Service, and very specifically suggest a model for what a Service, in the context of an IT Service Catalog, needs to contain from a definitional sense.
2. We will answer the question of how an IT Service Catalog makes a difference. We will highlight what makes a Service Catalog effective and relevant, and what business value can be expected and achieved.
3. We will explore how an IT Service Catalog and SLM processes are effectively implemented. We will discuss key roles, integration with key ITIL processes and the relationship of the Service Catalog with IT Service Management tools.
4. We will draw upon our collective experience of implementing IT Service Catalogs to answer the question of how they can enable the broader transformation of an IT organization that runs more like a business.

1.6 Case study

A leading Fortune 500 company recognized the limitations of its internal service processes as the corporation rapidly extended its worldwide operations. Faced with the realization that its existing organization, practices, processes and systems could no longer keep pace with the growth and demands of the business, the company launched a Service Catalog initiative as the cornerstone of a multi-phase initiative to transform its organization.

Phase One (starting with an End User focus)

During phase one of the project, more than 100 of the services most often requested of IT by its End Users were defined and published in an actionable Service Catalog – providing End Users with a single web-based catalog for ordering services. The results? Improved employee productivity by eliminating more than 1 million hours in time spent waiting for services, an annual cost savings of approximately $1.5 million, and a three-year ROI of more than 300%.

Phase Two (expanding to address Business Customers)

Leveraging the success and experience gained in phase one of the project, the team is now engaged with a broader initiative to add a Business Customer-focused layer to its Service Catalog, designed to support evolving relationship management and SLM roles and processes. This initiative includes the ability to selectively source certain services with external providers.

The business challenge

With an employee base of over 70,000 and an annual growth rate exceeding 15%, the demand for internal services at this Fortune 500 corporation had grown along with the business. The volume and range of requests for services continued to expand each month. However, the existing service delivery processes were inefficient, unmanageable and getting worse by the day. For IT Service Requests, in particular, the labor-intensive process was unwieldy and expensive:

- End Users submitted a form with their request for service;
- An eight-person administrative team received the requests;
- The administrators processed and routed requests to the appropriate IT staff or outsourced service teams;
- Any pertinent information missing from the original request meant that the IT representative would need to backtrack, find the appropriate requestor, and clarify the problem.

41% of services were delivered late (according to internally defined metrics of what on-time meant). End Users had no visibility into the status of their Service Requests, resulting in additional inquiries to determine when each service might be completed. The backlog in requests for IT Services alone resulted in more than 3 million hours of wait time each year (hours spent effectively waiting in line for needed services). To keep up with the needs of the business, and the increasing volume of services demanded by the employees, the IT Service organization had to find a better solution.

Running IT more like a business

The company recognized that inefficient service delivery operations were creating an expensive, unnecessary tax on corporate productivity. The problem manifested itself in a number of ways, including duplication of efforts, re-work or re-delivery of services, ineffective scheduling of service delivery teams, and employee dissatisfaction with internal services. To keep pace with the business, the service teams needed to find ways to deliver those services on-time and more cost-effectively.

The company articulated and embarked on a project to define and publish a web-based Service Catalog that could automate the entire Service ordering, approval and delivery cycle, by enabling self-service for employees as well as streamlined processes for service delivery teams. In addition management needed a solution to track and manage key service performance metrics such as on-time delivery and the cost per service delivered.

The goal was to run IT like a stand-alone business – with greater visibility and control of costs and quality of service.

The Service Catalog delivers

Leveraging a commercial, off-the-shelf Service Catalog solution, within 10 weeks the team had a Service Catalog up and running with 100 IT Services – providing a single web-based point of contact for employee Service Requests. The solution was integrated with other enterprise systems (e.g. LDAP, Single-Sign-On and Service Desk ticketing) to ensure a seamless and automated service delivery experience. In the following months the company deployed an additional 400 service staff and all requests for IT, telecommunications, security, and facilities services are now ordered and processed through the Service Catalog, which became the most often accessed point on the company's corporate intranet.

Lower costs and improved service quality

With the implementation of an End User focused Service Catalog as its phase one, the company has seen tangible and immediate benefits. The average cycle time for service delivery was reduced by more than 30%. On-time delivery of services increased from less than 60% to greater than 90%. And these results continue to improve: the cycle time on requests for new laptop PCs was recently reduced by more than 50%. The impact on employee productivity has been substantial, eliminating an estimated 1 million hours each year in time that employees wait for internal services.

Productivity of the service delivery teams improved as well, as service staff members are better able to set priorities and manage their workloads. Utilization of existing service delivery staff increased by 20%, and six service administrators were reassigned – resulting in approximately $300,000 in annual, recurrent savings. Service delivery processes have been streamlined and manual efforts are now automated. On average, the company reduced the cost of service delivery by 37%, or $42 per Service Request.

There are intangible benefits too. Employees are happier with the quality and timeliness of services they receive. By ordering from a catalog of standardized services, employees submit a clear and complete Service Request the first time – eliminating follow-up clarification calls and emails with service staff. Proactive notifications and online status updates keep employees informed of delivery status and expected timing. Real-time management reports provide key metrics to indentify bottlenecks, improve quality, shorten delivery cycles and even pinpoint services that may be better performed by external service providers.

Results that count

The company has calculated a cost savings of approximately $1.5 million annually, and a three-year ROI of more than 300%. End User Service Requests get handled faster and with fewer errors, increasing overall corporate productivity. Service teams can accomplish more with the same or fewer resources. Service executives can demonstrate the value of internal services to the Business Customer and rapidly align service delivery offerings.

Perhaps more important than any particular benefit is the renewed trust and credibility that the IT organization generated for itself in the eyes of its Business Customer partners. Having established that it can effectively and efficiently manage the day-to-day Service Request processes, the IT organization was given a broader charter to engage with the business not simply as a Cost Center that needed to be managed, but as a partner in the operations of the business. The success of phase one has led to a more ambitious phase two that seeks to expand the role of the Service Catalog in the operations of the company.

2

IT Services

As IT organizations evolve into a Service Delivery model it is important to understand where the industry has come from and how Technology Management differs in focus from Service Management. Over the last 20 years IT planning, strategy, recruitment, skills training, and reward and incentive programs have focused on developing centers of technology excellence. Individuals are hired and trained to hone their technology skills to optimize and reduce cost around the use of new technology innovation. However, for the most part education about the business perspective was ignored. Nowhere is this clearer than the fact that most computer science degrees have until recently been purely technology-focused and have little or no focus on teaching general business principles.

This training and hiring model results in technology domains where the technology components are managed in artificial isolation from each other. In a technology-focused IT organization there is little or no information available about which business processes are supported by which components.

Evolution of a service mentality starts with the awareness that a rudimentary responsibility of IT is the understanding of how any given critical IT component enables or disables a business process. Until this is known it is difficult to claim that IT is aligned to business goals. This initial understanding of risk begins to establish the need to maintain the relationship between IT components which ultimately are assembled into IT Systems and services. The definition and presentation of these services are presented as a structured portfolio of services found within the Service Catalog.

In summary, technology management is focused on the cost-optimization of technology domains, whereas a Service Management organization is focused on how technology components or professional activities are assembled together as IT Services which support the enablement of business processes. If the premise that a technology focus is not sufficient for business enablement and creates business risk is accepted, than it is logical to assume that an IT organization must understand itself as a service provider with a goal of business enablement and optimization.

The logical place to start this journey is first to understand of the business processes that IT Services support. Without this core understanding IT tends to try and define services from the bottom up instead of the top down. This technique is doomed to frustration and must be reversed. To understand how business processes are supported by IT Services the following approach is recommended.

■ 2.1 Steps for defining IT Services

The following section defines the logical and sequential steps to define a list of IT Services. Those steps are:
1. Define major business processes
2. Define enabling IT Services
3. Map IT Systems to IT Services
4. Map IT components to IT Systems
5. Service Based Costing

Step 1 - Define the Business Processes
The most appropriate way to define IT Services is from a business or customer perspective. To determine this, IT must understand how it facilitates the business in enabling the various business processes. The place to start this activity is to define what the business processes are. The following model (figure 2.1) is taken from the ITIL version 1 book *Understanding and Improving (1996)*. This model breaks the business processes down into four major categories.

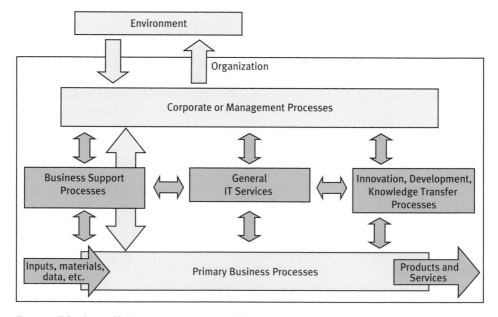

Figure 2.1 IT Services and business processes, source: OGC

- Primary business processes: Represent the main activities at the core of the organizations business model. For example:
  - Banking: Check Processing, Account Management, Mortgage Services, Internet Banking and Trading
  - Utilities: Power Generation and Distribution, Maintenance
  - Oil and Gas: Deep Water Drilling, Pipeline, Refining, Retail
- Support Processes: Represent the business processes that are used by all other business units such as:
  - Human Resources
  - Finance
  - Enterprise Procurement
  - Legal
  - Facilities
- Innovation Processes: Represent processes that position the organization and products within the market such as:
  - Marketing
  - Research and Development
  - Corporate Communications
  - Sales
- Management Processes such as:
  - Strategic Planning
  - Market Intelligence
  - Enterprise Risk Management

Each of these categories typically represent business groups that utilize both a set of general IT Services as well as application-based services which are uniquely used by specific business units to enable their business process areas. In turn most major business processes such as Financial Management have sub-processes such as Payroll. The first step in developing a customer-facing Service Catalog is the definition of all major business processes and sub-processes. This is a requirement in order to understand the next step, which is to map application and general IT Services to each of these primary business process areas.

Step 2 - Defining IT Services

In order to understand how to define customer-facing IT Services it is necessary to first define what an IT Service is. According to ITIL best practices the following definitions can be understood:

IT Service: One or more technical or professional IT capabilities which enable a business process. An IT Service exhibits the following characteristics:
- Fulfills one or more needs of the customer;
- Supports the customer's business objectives;
- Is perceived by the customer as a coherent whole or consumable product.

Note: By this definition a service is a capability, not a technology solution or vertical domain such as a server environment or a business application.

IT System: An integrated composite that consists of one or more of the processes, hardware, software, facilities and people, that provides a capability to satisfy a stated need or objective. An IT System:
- Is a collection of resources and configuration items or assets that are necessary to deliver an IT Service;
- Is sometimes referred to as a Technology Solution.

Note: The technology system is the complete composite of IT components from various domains which when brought together in a relationship represent a value-added technology solution; for example, a Local Area Network or an application system such as an Enterprise Resource Planning. A system is not referring to the application as a stand-alone element but to all of the components which build the complete solution (application, databases, servers and middleware, etc).

Configuration Item (CI): A component of an IT infrastructure that is part of an IT System. CIs may vary widely in complexity size and type – from a document or policy to an entire system or a single module or a minor hardware component.

Technical and Professional Services: When defining IT Services it is necessary to understand that there are two basic types of services that IT provides. These two types can be loosely classified as either 'Technical' or 'Professional' services.

A 'Technical Service' is defined as a technology-based capability that the customer consumes or uses in order to facilitate a business process or function. Technical services can be further understood as either application services or infrastructure services.

Examples of Technical Services are:
- General Infrastructure services such as:
  - Messaging/Email
  - File/Print
  - Network or Internet access
  - Office or desktop productivity
  - Voice Communications
  - Application Hosting
  - Storage Management
- Application-based services such as:
  - Financial Management Systems
  - HR Support
  - Power Generation Applications
  - Refining and Control Systems

Note: It is best practice to name the application-based service as closely as possible to the name of the business process it supports. This will be a critical step in understanding the business impact of IT Service or component failure.

The benefit of aligning the IT Service names with Business Processes is that it improves understanding for both the customer and IT staff on how technology is aligned to meet business objectives.

A 'Professional Service' is defined as the value-added activities that IT staff provide in order to support, maintain, monitor or ensure the consistent and reliable delivery of the technical services. Examples of Professional Services are:
• IT Architecture & Engineering
• IT Security
• IT Support
• Project Management Services
• IT Consulting
• Application Development and Enhancement Services

Note: It is very important that the IT organization takes the time to define professional services, since in most organizations 60% or more of the annual IT budget is spent on these services. If these services are not defined, these costs are reported as a non-value-added overhead. In summary the organization that does not define as many valued-added professional services as possible looks very fat when considered as an outsourcing option.

IT Services versus IT Processes: As discussed in this section the definition of IT Service represents the intelligent bundling of technology components and professional capabilities into IT Services which support Business Units and their corresponding processes (see figure 2.2). However, in the same manner that the Business Units have processes to accomplish and deliver to business goals, IT also has processes which exist for the sole purpose of supporting and delivering IT Services to its business partner.

As part of the movement towards a standard, regulated approach to the delivery of IT Services, there is a growing recognition that there is a benefit and perhaps even a requirement to apply internationally recognized best practice standards to the management of IT processes. The identification, selection and adoption of these standards is a part of the developing role of IT Governance. Where process models such as COBIT can provide a scope of what elements need to be in place, it is necessary to strategically select a collection of best practice frameworks covering the various areas of IT management to understand the requirements at a level of detail which can be executed.

The following are commonly used models adopted to satisfy governance requirements:
• Application Lifecycle Management: Capability Maturity Model (CMMI)
• Service Management: ITIL

- Security Management: ISO 17799
- Computer Operations and Data/LAN: Electronic Telecommunications Map (ETOM)
- Quality Management: Six Sigma/ISO
- Project Management: PMI or PRINCE2

Each of these best-practice process frameworks work in collaboration to deliver high-quality, consistent and reliable services to the business function.

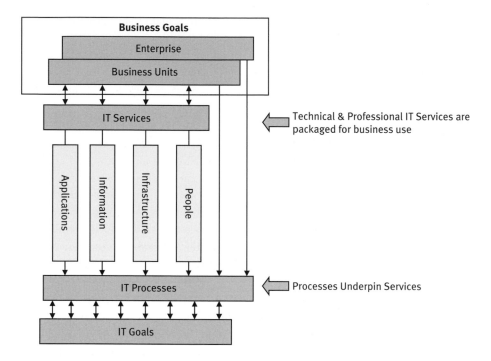

Figure 2.2 IT services versus IT processes

Step 3 - Map IT Systems to IT Services

The next step in this process comes more naturally to technical people since it involves defining and naming the IT Systems which the IT organization delivers and supports and mapping them to the IT Service definitions. Remember that an IT System is a collection of components required to deliver a Technology Solution to a customer. Often the IT System inherits the name of the primary application it is delivering. Another principle to keep in mind is that while there is a single IT Service definition, there are no limits to how many IT Systems can be mapped to this capability. Some examples of Service/Systems are listed in table 2.1.

When all IT Services and Systems have been defined by SLM, this information is provided to Configuration Management to facilitate the design of the CMDB Object Model and to Financial Management for the development of the Service Based Costing and Billing Models.

IT Service	IT System
Email	MS Exchange
	Lotus Notes
Shared Infrastructure	Data / LAN
	Voice
	Storage Management
HR Management	PeopleSoft
	Payroll

Table 2.1 Some examples of Service/Systems mappings

Step 4 - Map IT Components to IT Systems

Once IT Services have been defined and documented the next step is to leverage the Configuration Management process to model those services within the CMDB. Through object and data modeling techniques, a database of CIs can be created to present both a business service view as well as a technology view of how CIs are related in order to support business processes. In effect the ultimate goal of Configuration Management is to facilitate the creation of a real-time virtual model of the IT environment in relation to how it supports and delivers IT Services to Business Customers.

Configuration Management objective

Configuration Management provides a logical model of the infrastructure or a service by identifying, controlling, maintaining and verifying the versions of CIs in existence.
The goals of Configuration Management are to:
- Account for all the IT assets and configurations within the organization and its services;
- Provide accurate information on configurations and their documentation to support all the other Service Management processes;
- Provide a sound basis of data other processes such as Incident, Problem, Change, IT Service Continuity and Financial Management.

Configuration Management is an important part of the ITIL Service Management framework. It serves as the central hub for information sharing and collaboration.

Configuration Management IT Service Data Modeling

In order to model IT Services, an Object and Data Model must be developed to illustrate how different CI types are represented, their attributes and their connecting relationships. The data model dictates how IT Services are mapped in the CMDB. Without the inclusion of the IT Service structure in the CMDB, the database is of use only to technology groups and does not supply important data on business use and impact.

To use an analogy:
If the infrastructure is the puzzle and the CI the puzzle piece, then the Configuration Management Object Model design is the picture on the puzzle box.

Just as it is difficult to build a puzzle without the picture, it is difficult to understand how various CIs fit into a service architecture without the Object Model (fig. 2.3 provides an example Object Model).

Some key benefits derived from this model are:
• An understanding of how CIs within the scope of the process relate to IT business services;
• How direct and indirect asset costs are related to IT Services;
• How Availability figures relate to individual CIs, groupings of CIs and overall Service Availability targets;
• Which CIs facilitate multiple IT Services;
• Prioritization of CIs in relation to business criticality and function.

For each of the IT Business Services and technical IT Systems defined by the SLM Process there will be a record created in the CMDB within the logical structure. Once this structure is built within the tool it will remain relatively static and will not change drastically unless a new service is introduced to the environment.

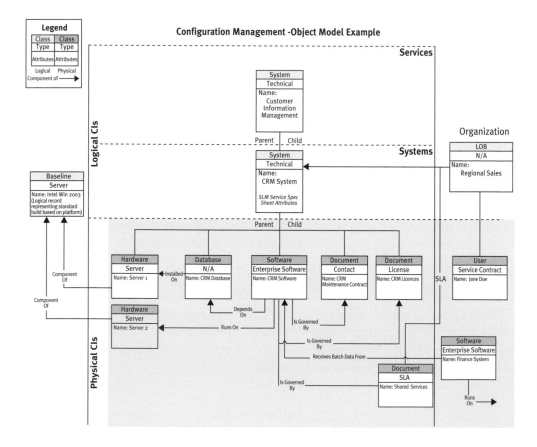

Figure 2.3 Configuration Management Object Model Example

Step 5 – Service Based Costing

A logical extension of the service structure is the development of a service-based costing model. When services are defined in the catalog it becomes necessary to align the costing mechanisms for how IT provides visibility into budget and accounting practices. Traditional Cost Center accounting tries to establish ownership for individual IT components to the business units which use them. The complexity of this model is that there are very few assets which are used exclusively or actually owned outright by a specific business unit.

Service-based costing takes a different approach. Its goal is to completely cost all services discretely in relationship to their direct, indirect and overhead allocation. Following this step decisions are made as to which services will be presented directly to the business client and which ones will be bundled as component or indirect services.

For example, an application service supports Mortgage accounts. As part of the Mortgage service a business chooses to allocate a certain percentage of the following indirect services:

• Hosting
• Storage Management
• Security
• IT Service Continuity
• IT Support
• Network

The total cost of the Mortgage service would include 100% of direct costs, an allocation of indirect and a fair percentage of true overhead (see figure 2.4).

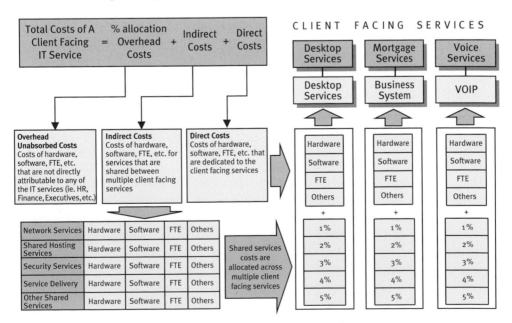

Figure 2.4 Service Based Costing example

The starting place for this process comes from the service structure found within the Service Catalog.

2.2 Who's on first? Start with the Service Catalog

With a view of how the CMDB and the Service Catalog relate, the next question is, where to start? The answer depends on the specific pain being resolved and the level of maturity of an organization.

If persistent problems in keeping key applications available and maintaining a basic level of support is the concern, then solve that first; a focus on Incident and Change Management processes may be the right thing. For most organizations, however, it makes sense to start with the Service Catalog early in an IT Service Management program. This could be as simple as a Service Catalog that maps to an inventory of applications. Think of this as a first phase catalog. It may include elements such as descriptions, service level options and included services, but need not initially include detailed information related to component services, pricing, costs and so on.

This first phase catalog is needed because the structure of the CMDB and the relationships need to make sense from the perspective of a service, and a service is always defined from the point of view of a customer. Defining services has to come first. This drives the structure of meaningful relationships which will then inform the CMDB.

Starting the other way around and trying to create the service from the CIs upward will not work. It is like trying to construct a meal for a restaurant by documenting the relationship between kitchen appliances. It will not succeed. Start with a menu of offerings (the catalog), which then drives the procurement of ingredients, the assembly of recipes and infrastructure of the kitchen.

The benefits of starting with a Service Catalog are several:
1. Rather than trying to reconcile thousands of CIs and attributes, start with the business view of the service and focus on just those aspects that are relevant.
2. It will make the CMDB project more relevant and visible to the business because IT will be able to paint a picture that aligns with its concerns in a language it can understand.
3. One of the CMDB's goals is to support effective Change processes that ultimately reduce down-time in operations by taking into consideration relationships between different items before changes happen. By enabling the IT organization to standardize the IT infrastructure on a controlled set of standardized services, the Service Catalog serves to reduce the complexity of the infrastructure that needs to be mapped in the CMDB and managed via Change processes.
4. Implementing a catalog first reduces project risk. An enterprise CMDB project is a multi-year effort and could easily devolve into a very IT-centric technical project which,

by the time it is complete, may no longer align to services the customers care about. Starting with the Service Catalog ensures that the CMDB project remains aligned with the customer's concerns.

5. Finally, there are issues of compliance and financial reporting to consider. SOX and other regulations in this vain, are bringing a new focus on risk management. In the next few months, the CFO will be asked for some simple reports – stuff that surely is already available. And, the CFO will say, "No problem go talk to …" You? Your boss? There will be an auditor asking for documentation regarding which businesses consume which services. They will be concerned with how costs are allocated depending on service consumption. Is a Business Unit underpaying to make results look good? The Service Catalog will be the key lens through which IT activities and costs will be examined.

3

Service Offerings, Agreements and Service Requests

Section 2 laid out a five-step process for defining an organization's IT Services, with the aim of developing an understanding of deployed IT Services and their relationship to both Business Processes and underlying IT Systems and Configuration Items. The challenge today is that the user experience and the technology-enabled business processes of the company are supported by vast arrays of technological devices, software components and third-party services, which must all operate concurrently to deliver an expected IT Service reliably.

The IT world has become more networked, the software stacks have acquired more layers of abstraction (application servers, database, web servers, business intelligence, etc.), and devices have proliferated (mobility is going to double the number of devices per employee). The result is that it is easy to lose the relationship between an IT Service and its business value. The IT Service does not live in a machine or a software package. It is distributed across hundreds of devices and software components.

While we are not futurists, we can safely predict this: there will be more data, more devices, more software, new stacks and new dependencies. As our organizations become more networked and adopt concepts like WIKIs, blogging and web 2.0 mashups, it will be harder and harder to figure out where an IT Service starts and ends.

In parallel, then, with efforts to discover, understand and map the dependencies among IT Services, IT Systems and CIs, we believe it equally important to develop an abstraction above the IT Service, what we call a Service Offering, that shields this level of complexity from the Business Customer, enables the advancement of Customer Relationship Management practices and processes, and lays the foundation for effective Service Request management. This design and definition of Service Offerings must be done from the customer perspective to succeed in escaping the seemingly invincible complexity of the IT infrastructure that threatens to slowly swallow time and focus.

■ 3.1 Services from the perspective of the customer

A definition of service from the Merriam-Webster Online Dictionary:

Main Entry: ¹**ser•vice**
Pronunciation: 'ser-vis'
Function: *noun*
Etymology: Middle English, from Anglo-French servise, from Latin *servitium condition* of a slave, body of slaves, from *servus slave*
1 a : the occupation or function of serving <in active *service*> **b :** employment as a servant <entered his service>
2 a : the work performed by one that serves <good *service*> **b :** HELP, USE, BENEFIT <glad to be of *service*> c : contribution to the welfare of others d : disposal for use <I'm entirely at your *service*>
3 a : a form followed in worship or in a religious ceremony <the burial *service*> **b :** a meeting for worship -- often used in plural <held evening *services*>
4 : the act of serving : as **a :** a helpful act <did him a *service*> **b :** useful labor that does not produce a tangible commodity -- usually used in plural <charge for professional *services*> **c** : SERVE
5 : a set of articles for a particular use <a silver tea *service*>
6 a : an administrative division (as of a government or business) <the consular *service*> **b :** one of a nation's military forces (as the army or navy)
7 a : a facility supplying some public demand <telephone *service*> <bus *service*> b : a facility providing maintenance and repair <television *service*>
8 : the materials (as spun yarn, small lines, or canvas) used for serving a rope
9 : the act of bringing a legal writ, process, or summons to notice as prescribed by law
10 : the act of copulating with a female animal
11 : a branch of a hospital medical staff devoted to a particular specialty <obstetrical *service*>

Stepping back from IT Service's technical definition, the word service is overloaded with many meanings when it is applied to IT. There are web services to get data, DSL services for Internet access, SLAs, service support processes, business services and so on. How is it that these are all called services? For a term so commonly used, it certainly seems confusing. Before going further it is important to establish the definition of what a service is for this book. Generally speaking:

> *A service is the coordinated performance of one or more activities by one or more people on behalf of somebody else for their benefit.*

By this definition a service is more than products consumed, but includes the related activities of people, processes and tools that together deliver an integrated service. Referring to our collective experiences, let us explore what we mean through a couple of simple examples:

■ **Examples:**

A restaurant is in the food service business. We go to a restaurant because they cook for us, they have expertise in cooking dishes we are not competent to prepare, and they wash the dishes. Alternatively, we could buy groceries and utensils, learn a recipe, and cook our meal, but when we go to a restaurant we are instead consuming an integrated service.

The same is true for electricity. We could buy a power generator, maintain it, run it, etc. Or, we could contract with the local utility to deliver electrical power at a certain price and availability. We let them construct cost-efficient generators, maintain them and perform all the necessary activities to ensure electrical service is available and that the lights go on when we flip the switch.

In both cases, we benefit from a service provider that bundles activities and materials into integrated services that we buy.

■ 3.2 Service Offerings

Extending this common-sense definition to the more precise definition of an IT Service Offering proposed here adds the notion of the roles of the service provider and the customer:

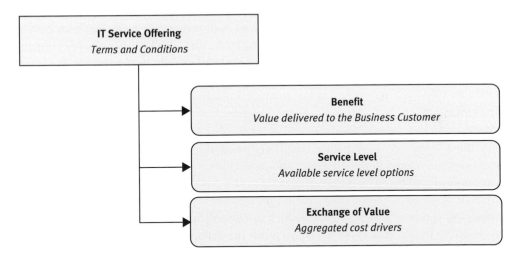

Figure 3.1 Service Offerings include the following elements: Benefit, Service Level and Exchange of Value

An IT Service Offering always has at least two participants: a service provider or performer offering to perform one or more tasks or activities to a certain specification, and a Business Customer willing to either accept the offered specification of the work or to request and specify the work.[3]

---

3 Our definitions of IT Services Offerings are derived from the work of Fernando Flores and Terry Winograd, who first tackled this notion in their book, *Understanding Computers and Cognition*.

In this expanded definition, a Service Offering is either offered to or requested by a Business Customer. Alternatively, it could be said that without a Business Customer a Service Offering cannot exist. The Business Customer needs to either specify the work or specify what work they want performed.

Going one step further, the specification of work within the context of a Service Offering needs to include the following in order to be considered effective:

> *Terms and conditions of the work to be performed, including benefit, expected service level, and an exchange of value for the work performed.*

Terms and conditions are the specifications that make a Service Offering finite, and set boundaries to the performance of the service and set the expectations of the benefit for the service. According to this definition, and as depicted in the following diagram, well-formed Service Offerings include the following elements: Benefit, Service Level and Exchange of Value.

Benefit

A Service Offering provides a benefit that helps or profits a customer. The Service Offering takes care of a concern, worry, want, requirement or need. It is this expectation of benefit that often causes the biggest disconnect between customers and performers. The customer expects a certain benefit, but the performer is focused on activities. The benefit of a Service Offering needs to be articulated clearly, quantified, and qualified in a way that both parties can objectively understand what is to be achieved by the service. Often benefits are implicit, which is sufficient for well understood services such as meals at a restaurant, but they need to be made explicit for complex IT Service Offerings.

Service Levels

Sometimes Service Levels are also implicit. At the fast food restaurant the food seems to arrive quickly enough. Why bother specifying when you want it? But behind the scenes franchisees are trained to deliver orders in one minute or less. They are measured and the franchise is graded based on those metrics.

Without the notion of a service level, explicit or implicit, a Service Offering is nonsensical. When will the food be delivered? What time is the installer arriving? How fast will the network be? How available will the application be? The customer needs to know. The performers need to know too. How long is delivery required? How reliable does the system need to be? The answer to these questions determines how things should get done.

For complex IT Service Offerings, service level explicitness is critical. Service levels for response, completion, communicating major milestones and breakdowns, availability and so on need to be defined and communicated or the service experience breaks down in acrimony, misunderstanding and distrust.

Exchange of Value

For a Service Offering to be considered more than an activity, it must have some value for the customer. A Service Offering without pricing and/or cost awareness is not sufficient. Without the exchange of value present, the customer has permission to ask for infinite service, and no way to fathom the value of the service for themselves.

Think about how price information helps us make decisions in daily life. The speed of cable or DSL, the restaurants we choose, the haircut we get, the home computer we have, and the cell phone plan we buy are all chosen on a price-versus-performance basis.

Pricing helps the customer make choices about the value of the service for them, by forcing a process of trying to figure out the benefit of the service in comparison to other activities they may be thinking of undertaking. Pricing helps shape demand and consumer behaviors. If IT wants to promote certain behaviors, pricing Service Offerings helps to indicate to the consumer the best value and which choice to make. For example, having a standard web-hosting service at levels of silver, gold and platinum is only useful if meaningful price comparison is possible.

This doesn't mean necessarily that a financial transaction need occur. It may be that a budget charge or published cost is sufficient, but there needs to be a clear financial awareness on the part of the customer and service provider. If a Service Offering is always free, without consequence to the customer, then the likelihood is that it will be over-consumed, with availability and quality service degrading in the process.

There are strong and weak forms of value exchange. In the strong form, there is a direct financial correlation between both customers and performers, benefit, and value. In a weak form, customers and performers are not connected directly. Examples of this occur when there is an intermediary buying the service or the value is non-financial. Either approach is valid, but service quality will be impacted negatively by the weak form.

■ Acid test: A Service Offering?

- Does it have a customer?
- Are there terms and conditions established?

Service Offerings empower the IT Organization

The practice most often missing in IT departments is having documented Service Offerings. When questioned as to why the response can be astounding. For example, "We don't want people to know what they can get," or "We don't want to be held accountable to commitments. We do it on a best effort basis."

If an organization doesn't have Service Offerings, then it is subject to whatever demands their customers care to invent. This will generate enormous variability and unpredictability in the skills and resources needed to deliver the service. Without Service Offerings it is impossible to drive standardization, which makes it impossible to drive costs down and reliability up.

One of the great benefits from creating Service Offerings is that it puts IT in the driver's seat. Offerings are actionable and demand initiative and involvement by customers. Offerings require talking with the customer about their needs, concerns and initiatives, forcing IT to think about marketing the offer and making it compelling and relevant to a customer. Offerings also force IT to think of the benefits they need to commit to delivering and how to deliver those benefits. When the value of IT activities are clear, and can be articulated in the context of Service Offerings, it is much easier to move the conversation with the business from one of managing costs to a meaningful value exchange.

■ 3.3 Relating Service Offerings and IT Services

In the prior sections a number of terms were defined. Now, let's begin to put the structures together. Figure 3.2 shows how a Service Offering relates to IT Services in the context of a simplified example of Desktop Management.

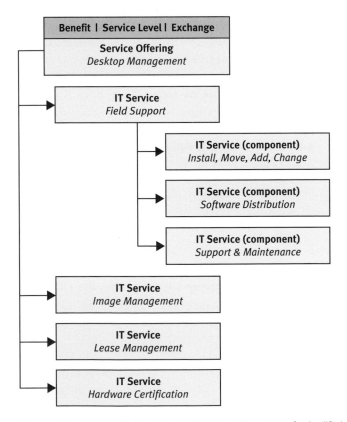

Figure 3.2 How a Service Offering relates to IT Services in the context of a simplified example of Desktop Management

Service bundles

As can been seen in figure 3.2, IT Services themselves can be bundles of other IT Services. The example shows that the IT Service of Field Support is itself a bundle of IT Services, including IMAC Services, Software Packaging and Distribution, Tier Two Hardware and Software Support and Maintenance, etc. With such a flexible taxonomy of nested IT Services, the difficult design question is determining where to draw the line. Or, in other words, how much detail is too much detail? Based upon our experience, an IT Service should be defined and made a visible component of the Service Offering if:

- Its cost is a meaningful percentage of the overall service cost;
- Its cost is variable through consumption;
- Showing the component service addresses a frequent question or common concern the customer may have;
- A competitor or external service provider includes it as an optional service in their offering;
- Calling it out will help to explain differentiation from a competitor;
- Having the service is required by law, regulation or compliance.

For example, at the time of writing, virus protection is a standard component of commercially available email services, while spam filtering is not yet widely adopted. This would lead to calling out spam filtering as a service component and probably making it optional. Distinctions between different levels of storage capacity should probably also be called out separately as storage accounts for a large percentage of email costs. Finally, you may want to call out compliance management and any record retention services you may need to provide. These add to the cost of the service. Calling them out helps explain why costs may be higher than a generic email service offered by a managed service provider.

Conversely, do not define and include an activity as an IT Service or component if the cost of the service is minimal. There is no need to name every aspect of what IT does. Similarly, don't include an activity if customers will not understand it or will resist paying for it. There is no need to generate confusion or consternation for the sake of developing a theoretically pure activity-based costing model.

IT Systems and resources

Resources are the elements of the service which need to be consumed or available for the service to be delivered satisfactorily. There are three classes of resources to consider:

1. IT Systems, encompassing devices and applications upon which the service is dependent;
2. Human Resources, including labor and skills;
3. Suppliers, including vendors and their underpinning contracts.

Vendor and human capabilities are extremely important within the context of IT. One of the aspects that makes IT Services complex is the need to coordinate people with specialized knowledge. Additionally, vendor resources are becoming increasingly critical to IT as organizations use managed services and on-demand systems.

This book's focus however, is on IT System resources. This is where the Service Catalog and CMDB link to each other. When attempting to understand the relationship between the two, a useful analogy can be drawn from manufacturing and the concept of the bill of materials.

A Bill of Materials (abbreviated 'BOM') describes a product in terms of its assemblies, sub-assemblies and basic parts. Basically consisting of a list of parts, a BOM is an essential part of the design and manufacture of any product.

BOMs contain hierarchical information with the master, or top-level BOM, describing a list of components and sub-assemblies. Take a PC, for example. The top-level BOM might list the shipping box, manual, packaging, packaging labels and the actual PC. The BOM for the PC itself is referenced in the top-level BOM and would contain its own list of sub-assemblies like power supply, motherboard, case, and so on.

This increasing level of detail continues for all sub-assemblies until it reaches its constituent parts (like resistors or processors), or modules that are out of the scope of the BOM (i.e. component parts that need not be managed independently, like the parts that make up a fan that is a self-contained input supplied by another manufacturer).

BOMs vary in their composition and usage throughout a product lifecycle. At various stages during the product lifecycle a bill of material defines products:
1.   As Designed
2.   As Ordered
3.   As Built
4.   As Delivered

In IT the Service Catalog and the CMDB play different yet complementary roles during the various stages of what can be thought of as the IT System product lifecycle. The Service Catalog becomes the source of record for the IT System: 'As Designed' and 'As Ordered'. The CMDB becomes the source of record for the IT System: 'As Built' and 'As Delivered'.

Figure 3.3 shows the relationship of IT Systems (As Designed) to IT Services and the Service Catalog.

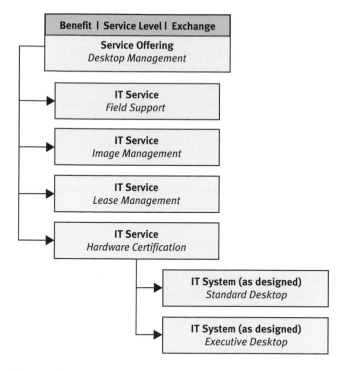

Figure 3.3 The relationship of IT Systems (As Designed) to IT Services and the Service Catalog

■ 3.4 Connecting to the Business Customer: Business Agreements

The IT Service Portfolio is the sum of all the Service Offerings the IT organization makes available to its customers. We call it a portfolio because it's primarily a financial tool for planning IT spending, forecasting demand, giving the executives a view into what is committed and a tool for enabling choices about investment in services.

Service Offerings are used to elicit Business Agreements from customers. Business Agreements are in turn how a Business Customer elicits performances from service groups. Based upon Business Agreements, service groups carry out processes which consume and change resources to deliver on the related Service Offering, according to the terms contained in the Business Agreement.

In other words, the Business Agreement is a Service Offering made actionable and relevant. It is the mechanism by which IT and its customers agree on what will be delivered, at what service levels and in what quantities. In turn it becomes the vehicle for budget and resource planning for both the customer and the performing service group.

Central to the effectiveness of Business Agreements is the definition and incorporation of business-relevant cost drivers. In a retail organization, the business may use several units of measure to manage operational efficiency and costs. These could be metrics such as per store, per square foot, inventory turns, profit margins, employee attrition or retention, transactions, and so on. It is very difficult for a manager to track measures like CPU cycles or availability metrics back to their business concerns. It is much easier for them to understand the impact and value of IT if cost drivers incorporated into Service Offerings and related Business Agreements are aligned with the metrics of the business.

The example above relates to retail, but every business has their own set of measures by which they manage their business. Airlines measure hours flown. software companies measure sales per employee, and semiconductor companies measure yield. The more aligned service costs are with the metrics of the business the easier it is for IT's customers to understand the value of IT and make the quality and cost trade-offs consequential to the business.

■   3.5 Connecting to the End User: Service Requests

One important aspect of the Business Agreement is that it provides the background context for implementing governance and control over Service Requests.

Service Requests are mentioned in ITIL version 2, but only in passing. Some people consider Service Requests to be simply a class of change management, or a Standard Request for Change. That may be, but it is a big class with its own unique attributes. The goal of Change Management is to minimize impact to the infrastructure through risk management. The goal of Service Request Management is to deliver to an End User a service according to the terms of a Business Agreement. Change Management is about putting structures in place to prevent careless changes that impact on the availability of IT Systems. Service Request Management is about making it easy for an End User to obtain the service they need to do their job.

Sometimes the Service Request is thought of in terms of "provisioning". Figure 3.4 shows the relationships connecting Service Offerings, IT Services and Service Requests.

A Service Request is where an End User meets the IT organization. To be effective, the definition of a Service Request, in addition to sharing many attributes of IT Service and Service Offerings, should include the following elements:
- Entitlement policies regarding who can receive the service and why;
- Authorization business rules;
- Configuration forms that guide the user in choosing, configuring and describing what is being requested;
- Service delivery plans, workflows and checklists;
- Status policies regarding when and how to communicate to the End User during the delivery process.

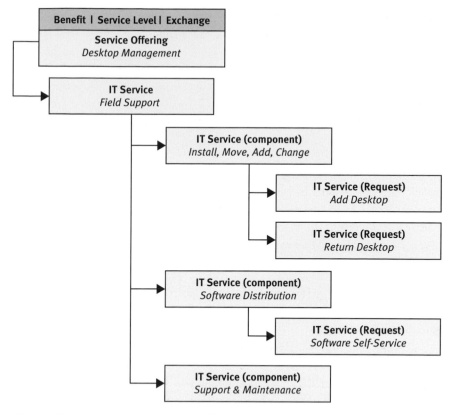

Figure 3.4 The relationships connecting Service Offerings, IT Services and Service Requests

■ 3.6 Putting it all together

The complete structure - linking Business Agreements to Service Offerings, IT Services, IT Systems and Service Requests - is depicted in figure 3.5.

The Service Catalog, then, is a nested set of Business Agreements, Service Offerings, IT Services, IT Service Components and Service Requests, which together relate to IT Systems and their related Configuration Items. Different views of the Service Catalog are relevant depending on the role and the needs.

A note on categories

Categories are important for a number of reasons. They serve to group similar services so they can be displayed in customer language on a portal, rolled up for reporting purposes, aggregated for budgeting and so on.

It's not important to have one category for one service. Multiple categories may be appropriate for each service. For example, the IT Service 'new laptop' may be have display categories for

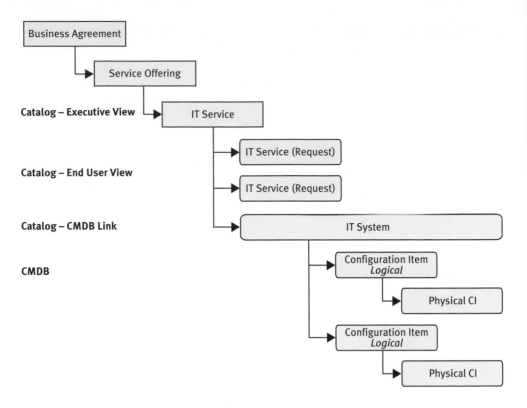

Figure 3.5 Linking Business Agreements to Service Offerings, IT Services, IT Systems and Service Requests

the Service Catalog such as hardware, desktop, personal computer and new employee set-up. For budgetary purposes, it may be placed under hardware. And, for organizational purposes, it may be placed under End User Computing.

We recommend the usage of at least four classes of categories:
• Display, for displaying services in a service portal.
• Reporting, for reporting services in different aggregations.
• Budgetary, for matching service expenses to the General Ledger or Cost Centers.
• Organizational, for understanding how services are delivered.

■ Example: Web Hosting

Let's imagine an IT department has a Service Offering called Web Hosting. The Catalog describes what is included, the price, how it is charged, and the rest of the elements specified in prior sections. The Service Offering would also document all the component IT Services and IT Systems ('as designed').

Let's say a marketing executive needs a new website for a new marketing promotion. The executive or their Relationship Manager goes to the Service Catalog, reviews the Web Hosting offering, determines that the 'silver' service level best meets his or her needs, and then proceeds to initiate a Business Agreement based upon this Service Offering.

This Business Agreement triggers provisioning and configuration to be carried out, such as ordering servers, deploying licenses and granting access to users, all of which are managed as a Service Request.

As the delivery process is building the system through either a workflow system or Change Management system, the CMDB CIs are being added or discovered, and reconciled. The CMDB now contains a new IT System that it will track and report the main elements back to the catalog system. The CMDB will then keep the actual consumption of storage and report it back in the context of the Business Agreement.

Once the web-hosting service is operational, the Service Catalog system plays a different role. Where before the catalog served a publishing and ordering function, it now manages a Business Agreement. Where before it documented "resources to be provided", it now links to the CMDB to show "resources being used and consumed".

The marketing executive can then go to their Service Portfolio and see all the different Business Agreements they may have consummated, together with actual cost and performance numbers, and the history of Service Requests made within the context of each Business Agreement. What does IT do for me? What does it cost? How well does it do it? These questions now disappear.

■ 3.7 Generating perceived Service Quality

The previous sections stretched the notion of a service from an IT System, based on technology components, to customer-centric IT Services and Service Offerings. For IT professionals this represents a challenge, as they are typically 'hard-wired' to think in terms of things such as servers, routers and databases, and not benefits, prices and value.

For an IT veteran the intangible nature of both IT Services and Service Offerings may at times seem vague or indescribable. In fact, there are distinct and observable characteristics that distinguish a service from a system.

1. Services are manufactured and consumed at the same time, and thus subject to failure and variability each time. It's difficult for service delivery personnel to store 'services' for future use and as such they are consumed as the customer uses them. Practically, this means that to ensure a reliable service to a customer, one must often over-supply capacity to deal with breakdowns and peak demand.
2. Services are heterogeneous. They vary from person to person, and by time and place. This means that two people getting the same service from the same person or group may have widely different experiences. This is one of the reasons why standardization of

services and communication of service levels are critical. Without explicit standards the customer is forced to create their own.

3. Customers judge the quality of service both by the *outcome* and the *process* of delivery. It's not enough to say that an application performs according to specification in the contract. One needs to consider the variety of what it takes for the customer to get what they perceive as the service: *Is it easy to gain access to the application? Are regulatory controls being enforced? Can I understand what I am paying for? Are my enhancement requests being dealt with as I expect?* All of this contributes to forming the customer's perception of the overall service.

4. A customer's *expectations* for service and their *perception* of the service delivered drive their opinion of service quality. When dining at a fast food restaurant, the customer expectation is to receive a standard offer at a low price, quickly. The customer doesn't expect great food or surprises, and would be unhappy to wait too long. Go to a four star restaurant and the expectations are completely different! The customer expects to be surprised by the food, delighted with the treatment, and yes, shocked by the prices. If the waiter brings the food in two minutes, it would be confusing, as it wouldn't match expectations. Most IT organizations, however, do not set clear expectations for services, yet wonder why their customers don't appreciate the quality of the IT Service. How could the customer appreciate it? They are left to create their own expectations in a domain that is incomprehensible to them.

5. Customers are the final judges of quality. Since services are intangible and can only be experienced, there is no objective third party or availability metric one can appeal to. It's the customer who determines quality.

6. Customers are often unable to understand what is required to deliver a service and thus have difficulty establishing its value. This is often why a customer buys a service in the first place; they don't know how to perform it, find that it is too complex or too costly for them to manage. Unfortunately, this means that they also have a hard time assigning costs or understanding complexity.

7. Services are abstractions used to 'hide' underlying complexities and details that may not be relevant to or understandable by the customer.

Perception drives quality of service

Putting all of the above together, services are activities that lead to customer experiences. Experiences are formed by perceptions that need to be managed to ensure a satisfactory experience. Since perception drives a customer's assessment of service quality, it is important to understand how perceptions are formed by the customer. There are ten different dimensions customers use to determine their dimensions of service quality (see figure 3.6).

For this section, we are indebted to the work of Valarie A. Zeithami, A. Parasuraman and Leonard L. Berry, who wrote *Delivering Service Quality: Balancing Customer Perceptions and Expectations* (Simon & Schuster, 1990). Their work describes each of these dimensions and their impact on a customer's perception of quality of service, as summarized in table 3.1.

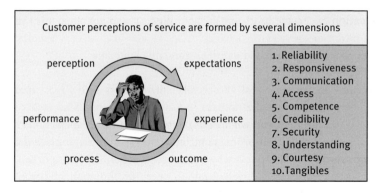

Figure 3.6 Customer perceptions of service are formed by several dimensions

1	Reliability	Does the organization make accurate and dependable promises?
2	Responsiveness	How willingly and promptly does the organization respond to my concerns?
3	Communication	Are personnel informed? Do they use the customer language? Do they listen to my concerns?
4	Access	How approachable and easy to deal with is the service provider?
5	Competence	Does the provider exhibit skills and knowledge? Can they perform competently?
6	Credibility	Are they trustworthy, honest, and believable?
7	Security	Is the service experience free of risk or danger? Am I in doubt about what will happen?
8	Understanding	Does the provider understand my needs and my situation?
9	Courtesy	Am I shown respect and consideration during the service delivery process?
10	Tangibles	Is the physical experience pleasant? Is the appearance suitable?

Table 3.1 Dimensions and their impact on a customer's perception of quality of service

Of the above dimensions, reliability seems to be the most important. There are entire enterprises that have defined themselves by the reliability of their service and the impeccable promises they make. FedEx, for example, promises that packages will get there by 10 am, guaranteed. It is not the cheapest way to send a package, but that promise allows businesses to schedule other activities more reliably, which has value beyond the relatively small cost of the package delivery. This case illustrates how understanding a customer's perception of value can change what people think of as a service.

The importance of reliability is why IT spends so much time and effort working to make sure systems are up and running, and available to users. Beyond reliability, however, IT organizations must also focus on the dimensions that generate perceived quality, noted above, if they are to be perceived as delivering quality services.

Since IT organizations are complex, a great amount of coordination and a higher level of communication are required to manage service delivery. Also, IT also uses a very specific technical jargon, so IT must be extra diligent and use the customer's language.

In fact, most customers do not understand what IT delivers, how to approach IT or what IT has to offer. They are not competent in the domain, nor should they be. This lack of knowledge results in a web of uncertainty, fear and apprehension - one where the customer's normal competencies don't work. These emotions cause the customer to eventually place the blame for that lack of understanding on IT. That is why even though reliability is important, the other dimensions need to be considered as well. Table 3.2 outlines the applicability of each dimension within the context of IT.

	Dimension	Applicability
1	Reliability	Applicability: Make specific promises, connect these promises to the service delivery, and allow the customer to see, on their own, that you are meeting these promises. Have a service-specific communication plan if you anticipate a breakdown. Watch out: If your are not sure of your reliability, call it out. Don't hide your service levels, otherwise you just give permission to the customer to invent their own.
2	Responsiveness	Applicability: Ensure email and prompt communication that is documented and acted on in the service. Don't worry about over-communicating. Watch out for: Fake responsiveness, like picking up a phone in five rings. Sure, it's needed, but what happens after that?
3	Communication	Applicability: Understand what the service does for the customer, what they use it for. Ensure the service is defined from the concerns of the customer and articulates benefits. Watch out for: Overtly technical language or metrics that the customer can't translate to their operational needs.
4	Access	Applicability: Publish a Service Catalog, have it online, searchable, categorized according to business processes, functions, roles or uses. Provide comparisons between services. Use entitlement instead of pure approval. Watch out for: Complicated forms, technical jargon and secret processes and criteria to get funding.
5	Competence	Applicability: Have Relationship Managers and Product Managers to bridge the gap between the underlying technical capability and the customer's business. concern. Organize IT from outside-in rather than inside-out. Watch out for: Not putting real authority behind your Relationship Managers and Product Managers.
6	Credibility	Applicability: Use the catalog to communicate breakdowns. Make clear performance promises. Acknowledge mistakes. Watch out for: Defining service levels in terms of tasks rather than outcomes, metrics of activities rather than benefits.

	Dimension	Applicability
7	Security	Applicability: Guide the customer to their service selection. Use examples. Don't be terse. More text is better. Provide link to other resources, and help make comparisons. Speak in terms of roles, functions, outcomes, benefits or business processes. Watch out for: Organizing a catalog by silo or domain.
8	Understanding	Applicability: Define services for specific roles, functions and/ or process. Don't worry if this leads to service proliferation. As long as the activities are recurrent, it's OK to have different ways to get the same service. Watch out for: Services defined purely from a technology view.
9	Courtesy	Applicability: Be specific in your language and on how to recover from a breakdown. Watch out for: Training employees to be courteous but not giving them power to actually address the customer's issue. Avoid service level descriptions that avoid responsibility.
10	Tangibles	Applicability: Meet the expectations set by high quality e-commerce portals, and match the experience customers are used to in the consumer world and web. Watch out for: Bad writing, unclear language and lack of graphics. Looking like a 10-year-old website.

Table 3.2 The applicability of each dimension within the context of IT

4

Implementing SLM

When considering where to start an ITIL initiative generally, and when to work on SLM processes in particular, there are many considerations that often lead to lengthy and philosophical debates. However, while a recommended sequence for process implementation can be considered relative for each organization, there are certain truths based on general ITIL principles. Based on logic and sequence, certain processes need to be in place and in a more or less mature state in order to support the introduction of others. For this reason process dependencies can be defined.

To start the discussion, there are two basic premises to consider:
1. IT's role is to support, control and manage defined IT Services for the business (Incident, Change and SLM).
2. Certain processes are business-facing while others occur behind the scenes (Incident, Change and SLM).

With these two considerations, one starts to see that the ITIL processes begin to take on a logical sequence. It is our experience that, regardless of company-specific factors, most organizations will start with the same processes for the following reasons:
1. Support of IT Services is a core and visible element of Service delivery.
2. Uncontrolled and unplanned changes have an adverse effect on Service delivery.
3. It is difficult to plan proactively unless it has defined what Services it provides and at what levels.

For this reason many organizations take a top-down and bottom-up approach to process implementation sequencing.

Starting from the premise that the basic support and control processes need to be in place to ensure that IT is doing the most basic of its tasks, it is logical to assume that many organizations start their ITIL process journey by making improvements to their Incident and Change processes.

Additionally, if it is understood that the processes of Service Management only exist for the purpose of supporting and delivering IT Services, then it also makes logical sense to understand what those services are. For this reason many companies will tackle the Service Catalog element of SLM at an early stage as well.

Contrary to popular belief and practice, the creation of SLAs is not the first step in the implementation of SLM. As indicated earlier (see "How to fail at SLM with SLAs" in chapter 1), there are two progressive levels for SLM implementation:
• Stage A: Service Catalog design and implementation of the processes and roles which support it.
• Stage B: The establishment of SLAs and Service delivery meetings.

Deliverables for Stage A:
1. The definition of technical and professional service capabilities provided to the business.
2. The ability to monitor the IT organization's capability to meet internal IT targets for service delivery.

Once IT Services have been defined and catalogued and the IT organization has developed the capability to consistently deliver and monitor services, agreements can be developed and signed off with the customer.

Deliverables for Stage B:
1. The development of consumption-based SLAs with individual customers or Lines of Business.
2. The establishment of regular service reports and continuous improvement programs.

■ 4.1 The SLM process

As discussed in the previous section, IT Services are supported and delivered by IT processes. However, both of these elements are delivered and managed as horizontal elements within a traditional command-and-control-based organization structure based on vertical IT silos or domains.

Just as it is necessary to establish management structures and roles within the traditional domains or departments, it is also a critical success factor to define management roles for both IT Services and Processes. Both require management, measurement and a focus on improvement. To quote an old saying: "What gets measured gets done!"

However, it is equally true that sometimes what is measured is the only thing that is done. Without the establishment of accountability and perhaps more importantly the measurement of objectives against this accountability, neither Services or Processes have much hope of being viewed as effective or efficient.

In reality what is actually occurring when an organization defines IT Services and Process roles is that two new virtual organizational structures are being established on top of the traditional domain-based silos. The end result of this is the establishment of a matrix organization where individuals within it have multiple lines of accountability and are constantly faced with the requirement to prioritize their time.

In this environment the process of SLM plays a critical role. The process and roles of SLM tie together the traditional silo-based organization and provide guidance and policy around resource prioritization.

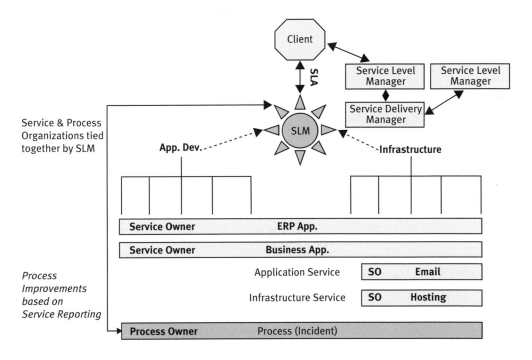

Figure 4.1 The process of SLM plays a critical role

In this model (figure 4.1) the relationship of IT as an enterprise function is front-ended by the SLM process. It is supported by the establishment of a Service Catalog from which the roles of SLM engage with, and negotiate, SLAs.

The key element of this relationship is that IT is presented as a single provider to the business partner. The process and its catalog provide a single face to the business from which it can expect the delivery of end-to-end services. Some of these services are application-based and directly support business processes, others are front- or back-office infrastructure services and still others are the provision of value-added professional services which support the delivery, maintenance and continuous improvement of the IT Service offering.

SLM, by its definition of IT Services, provides the critical business context and prioritization required by IT to ensure that its actions reflect the best interests of the stated goals of the business. The gathering of requirements and the establishment of business-facing service agreements drive the development and improvement of the processes which support them.

The SLM process has as its focus:
1. The establishment of business requirements;
2. The measurement of service delivery against this requirement;
3. The reporting of how these services are being delivered to the business partner;
4. The identification of where improvements need to be made within IT Services and or the processes which deliver them.

So, in essence SLM facilitates the definition and management of IT Services in collaboration with the management roles of both Services and Processes.

4.2 Roles of SLM

ITIL provides some context regarding the roles of SLM. In practice, however, most organizations require an expansion of the role which is called a 'Service Level Manager'. In this section the definition of the role of a Service Level Manager will be expanded upon, and will include definitions of the related roles of Service Delivery Manager and Service Owner.

Service Level Manager (aka Relationship Manager)

The Service Level Manager is responsible for the relationship between IT and the business. It is the Service Level Manager who is responsible for working with the business owner to understand requirements and to establish and document service agreements based on the catalog of services provided by IT. It is also the role of the Service Level Manager to develop and broker OLAs between IT groups to facilitate the delivery of end-to-end services. While ITIL calls this role a Service Level Manager, many organizations will use the term of Client Relationship or Account Manager. Semantics aside, the general purpose of this role is essentially the same.

In addition to the creation of SLAs, the overall role of the Service Level Manager includes the creation of customer-facing service reports which provide the Business Customer who is using the services with a perspective of how well the services are being delivered according to the promises and agreements made in the Service Catalog and SLAs.

These report cards or service dashboards are in reality roll-ups of the data coming from both services and processes at a level which is understandable by the business partner. In essence SLM extracts key data from multiple perspectives to provide this information (see figure 4.2).

Based on these reports meetings are held on a regular basis with the business partner. The resulting feedback is brought back to the service and process owners to direct areas of continuous improvement.

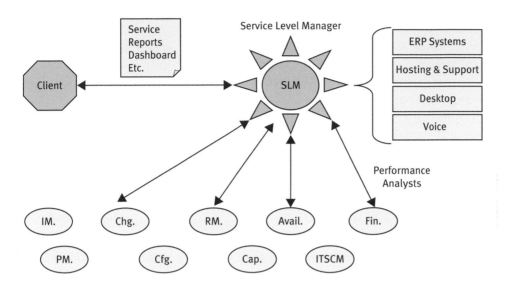

Figure 4.2 Service Reporting Model

From this perspective the process and roles of SLM are critical to the goals of quality and continuous improvement.

Service Delivery Manager (aka Product Manager)
The Service Delivery Manager is accountable for the strategic view of overall IT Service offerings as described by the catalog, and is responsible for the tuning and improvement of those services in order to ensure they continue to meet business needs. It is not uncommon to find a Service Delivery Manager as a direct report to the CIO. In some organizations this role is referred to as a Product Manager.

Services cut across silos and cross different functions. It is the Service Delivery Manager's role to assemble them into bundles that make sense to IT's customers. The Service Delivery Manager both leads and collaborates in defining, supervising and enhancing services to achieve the necessary levels of customer satisfaction, regulatory compliance and operational effectiveness. For most managed service providers this is a well understood and entrenched role. It is less common within corporate IT organizations today.

This role is responsible for defining both the specific services to be provided and the roadmap of future IT Services. This is done in conjunction with Service Level Managers, IT executive management and Service Owners. To do this, the Service Delivery Managers must own the definition of service levels, measures, bundles, resources, pricing and cost allocation. They are the ones who design the options between quality and cost from which the customer can then select. Service Delivery Managers are responsible for the competitiveness of their offer in the marketplace, which includes benchmarking their services against external providers and leaders in their industry.

Service Owner

The Service Owner is accountable for a specific service within an organization regardless of where the technology components or professional capabilities reside which build it. Service ownership is as critical to service management as establishing ownership for processes which cross multiple silos or departments.

To ensure that a service is managed with a business focus, the definition of a single point of accountability is absolutely essential to provide the level of attention and focus required for its delivery.

Much like a process owner the Service Owner is responsible for continuous improvement and the management of change affecting the services under their care. In both cases these horizontal roles are effective or not according to the level of empowerment given to the role by the executive of the IT organization. The Service Owner is a primary stakeholder in all of the IT processes which enable or support it. For example:

- Incident Management: Involved in or perhaps chairs the crisis management team for high-priority incidents impacting the service owned.
- Problem Management: Plays a major role in establishing the root cause and proposed permanent fix for the service being evaluated.
- Release Management: Is a key stakeholder in determining whether a new release affecting a service in production is ready.
- Change Management: Participates in Change Advisory Board decisions, approving changes to the services they own.
- Configuration Management: Ensures that all groups which maintain the data and relationships for the service architecture they are responsible for have done so with the level of integrity required.
- SLM: Acts as the single point of contact for a specific service, and ensures that the Service Catalog is accurate in relationship to their service.
- Availability and Capacity: Reviews technical data from a domain perspective to ensure that the needs of the overall service are being met.
- IT Service Continuity: Understands and is responsible for ensuring that all elements required to restore their service are known and in place in the event of a crisis.
- IT Financial Management: Assists in defining and tracking the cost models in relationship to how their service is costed and recovered.

■ 4.3 Service Catalog and IT Tools

The increased complexity and distribution of the IT environment has made the efficient management of the IT infrastructure and its services almost impossible without the aid of specialized tools. For the businesses to achieve its goals and objectives, IT needs to be strategically involved in helping to explore new opportunities for growth. To achieve true business alignment, IT must change its focus from traditional systems-management metrics towards an end-to-end service management model.

As organizations automate the processes that define, support, manage and control IT Services, ITIL is becoming the global standard for IT management best practices. Figure 4.3 represents the ITIL processes from a tool perspective.

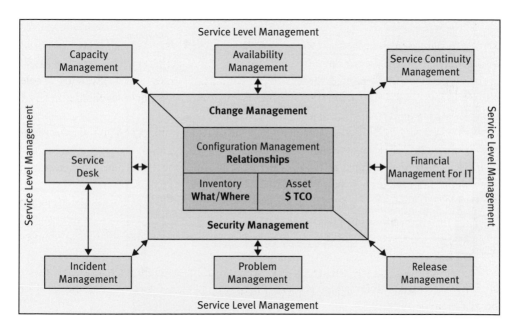

Figure 4.3 The ITIL processes from a tool perspective

As shown at the center of Figure 4.3, the process of Configuration Management has as its goal the management, and control, of key information provided to other IT processes. This data can be viewed from different perspectives such as:
• Inventory: What, where, who and how many?
• Asset: How much does it cost now and in the future?
• Configuration: What is related to what and how does it support or enable a business process?

Processes, such as Incident and Problem Management, focus on the support of IT Services. Security, Change and Release Management focus on the control, coordination and deployment of changes into the production environment.

Availability, Capacity, IT Service Continuity and Financial Management enable a day-to-day operational view, as well as the longer term tactical planning, modeling and costing.

Finally, SLM translates technology components to elements of IT Services and provides reporting, quality management and relationship management between the business and the IT organization.

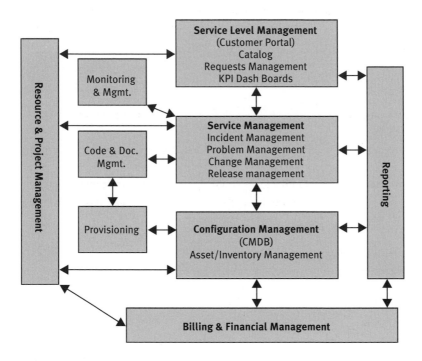

Figure 4.4 An integrated architecture of tools that support IT Service Management

Figure 4.4 represents an integrated architecture of tools that support IT Service Management. At the top of this stack we find the Service Catalog representing the customer portal. This portal fulfills three main functions:
1. It provides a comprehensive portfolio and description of services that support the engagement and negotiation of SLAs with Business Customers.
2. It also provides a platform for submitting and tracking requests for service against the defined portfolio of services.
3. The web-based catalog also provides an ideal location for reporting on the delivery of services as documented and agreed with Business Customers.

In essence an actionable Service Catalog provides an internal IT e-commerce portal for engaging with its internal Business Customers on both a Business Customer and individual user level.

Service Request and Change Management

An important integration to consider with the Service Catalog is the 'Service Request' process. At a high level, the Service Request process is similar to the Change Management process and is often considered as being equal to what ITIL calls a standard or pre-approved change (although in ITIL v3 the Service Request process is recognized as its own management process).

In many organizations the function of the Service Desk is to own this process and be accountable for the end monitoring of its fulfillment. The entry point of requests can be both manual as well as automated.
For example:
1. A user calls the Service Desk and makes a vocal request which is recorded as a Service Request record.
2. An email is sent to the Service Desk which is then translated into a Service Request record.
3. A link is provided on an internal company intranet to a self-service request form with a rudimentary list of options to select from.
4. A Service Catalog provides a structured and personalized list of defined Service Offerings to a customer or user. The user is presented the option within the catalog to request a new or modified service element.

The last scenario represents how the Service Catalog can be used to automate the Service Request management process.

Service Support classification

The various process frameworks for supporting and delivering IT Services define enterprise processes and workflows which ultimately end up as management records within IT tools. In order to support automation, integration and management reporting requirements it is necessary to develop common classification models for these processes. Otherwise, each process and tool is a stand-alone solution which produces data unique to its configuration. If IT Services and processes cross organizational structures and silos it stands to reason that the classification schemas represented in the various IT tools must be aligned. One critical classification that is required is a service classification which comes from the portfolio of services represented in the Service Catalog.

For example, a user calls the Service Desk and reports that they cannot access the IT Service called email. There may be several technical and non-technical reasons why this has occurred and a classification schema is required to capture the source and probable root cause. It is very possible that the technical classification schema may be updated several times during the lifecycle of the incident. However, the fact remains that, regardless of the source or cause of the incident, the user cannot access the email service.

For this reason workflow or process records such as Incident or Problem records need to be classified according to the following basic schemas:
- IT Service impacted (e.g. Financial Trading)
- Technical area of impact or change (e.g. Server Failure)
- Priority (e.g. Business Impact and Urgency)
- Closure code (likely cause of failure e.g. process – unauthorized change)

Likewise change and release require the following classifications:
- IT Service being changed (e.g. email)
- Technical area of change (e.g. database update)
- Change and Release risk type (e.g. major, medium, minor, emergency)
- Change and Release success status (e.g. successful, backed out, failed)

Ultimately a report can be generated that demonstrates service disruption or change against the IT Service or technology component, and likely root cause and Business Unit affected.

Delivering customer-facing Service Reports

An organization that is focused on continuous improvement and has adopted a culture of measurement will be focused on producing metrics from three different perspectives:

1. Technical metrics which detail the throughput, efficiency and availability of technology components.
2. Service Reports which are customer-centric roll-ups of the technology metrics which provide the basis of service availability and performance according to the defined offering or SLAs.
3. Process reports which provide information about the health, maturity, value and efficiency of IT processes which support the delivery of IT Services.

All three reports types are required by different audiences in the service delivery and consumer models. However, most of the data being collected is for the purposes of IT management and improvement. It is the role of SLM to take all three data sources listed above to create customer-centric reports and service dashboards that provide a Business Customer with the perspective of how services are being delivered, currently and historically, according to the agreement recorded in the Service Catalog and specifically within SLAs.

The online Service Catalog is the logical place to present the customer-facing roll-up of these metrics.

5

Defining The Business-Focused Service Catalog

Now that the definitions for both a service and SLM are identified, it is time to turn our attention to why the definition of IT Services, Service Offerings and Service Requests is a relevant and meaningful exercise. In other words, for what purpose are we proposing that organizations engage in the exercise of cataloging their services? The answer is that Service Catalogs can and should drive value in the organization on multiple levels. From our perspective an effective Service Catalog should be:

- Constitutive, in that it defines what IT does and does not do, and on what terms;
- Actionable, in that it provides the means by which IT and its customers coordinate and conduct business;
- Governing, in that the key terms, conditions and controls defined in the Service Catalog are integrated into the service delivery processes of the organization.

■ 5.1 The constitutive nature of the Service Catalog

By choosing the word 'constitutive' to describe one attribute of an effective Service Catalog, we purposefully intend to invoke the notion of a constitution of sorts for IT:

"We the people (of IT), in order to form a more perfect union (alignment with the business), establish justice and ensure domestic tranquility..."

The basic act of setting to paper what it is that the IT organization does, and just as importantly what IT doesn't do (in the form of a Service Catalog), provides the structure around which a set of loosely related technical and functional IT silos can be organized into an effective and integrated IT organization. A good Service Catalog becomes the source of truth or cornerstone for defining what it is that IT is in business to do, who its customers are, and how the different parts of IT need to be organized to work together to deliver value to those customers. If the

CMDB is the system of record for what IT did, then the Service Catalog becomes the system of record for what IT does.

Drawing again from the restaurant analogy, the contents of the Service Catalog define the kind of restaurant and what customers can expect. Does it serve Chinese or Italian food, or both? Is it a self-service buffet or are white linens and candlelight provided? Is it cheap and fast or expensive and high quality? Of course, there are restaurants of all sorts, and which one consumers select depends on individual tastes and concerns at that particular time. Similarly in the world of IT, there are many possible ways to 'prepare and serve' IT Services. The question is determining which styles of services are right for a particular organization at a particular time. The power of a well articulated and communicated Service Catalog is that it gives an IT organization a way to dialog with its customers to find the mix of service breadth and quality that best fits the needs of the business. The Service Catalog, then, becomes the vehicle through which the elusive goal of business and IT alignment is hashed out.

Beyond business and IT alignment, knowing the expected services, the level of quality and the price allows an IT organization to optimize its back-end delivery processes. It is important to ensure that what is optimized is in line with what the organization's customers value. The Service Catalog should provide the mechanism to define and agree with customers what it is that they want so that the IT organization can optimize its delivery processes and organization to provide just that.

The Service Catalog is, then, a critical first step in ensuring that IT Services align with the business unit's needs. By establishing a standard set of service offerings, with associated service levels and costs – and then publishing that information to the internal customers of IT – the IT organization can leverage market forces to manage demand for services. IT can become more demand-driven, based on informed customer requests for pre-defined Service Offerings, and thus improve alignment.

A customer-focused IT Service Catalog provides the basis for a balanced, business-level discussion on trade-offs regarding the cost and quality of service. The result is an ongoing conversation between the customer and the service provider that delivers greater value to both sides, ensuring higher customer satisfaction and superior SLA compliance. Customer demand then drives actions and choices and thereby produces alignment.

■ 5.2 The actionable nature of the Service Catalog

One complaint often heard from IT organizations that are earnestly attempting to define their services and related delivery processes around what matters most to its customers, is that teams charged with building a Service Catalog have difficulty getting the business to engage with them on defining and creating it. One such team told us once that they could serve 'champagne and caviar' at brown bag lunches and still not be able to get the interest of the true Business Customer.

The reality is that while IT Services are becoming ever more critical to the day-to-day functioning of business, most Business Customers don't want to think about most IT Services. They want it to be like the electricity in the building. It should just work. And, like the electricity costs, not hit their budget. They don't have the time nor the inclination to attend meetings to talk about the trade-offs between availability metrics and costs, for example. IT is most likely to only have their Business Customers attention when they are looking to IT to deliver a new project or service, or when they are pulling together their budgets and looking for ways to squeeze money out of their fixed cost allocations. Similarly, End Users tend only to seek out IT when they have a breakdown – when they either need something to do their job or when something they need to do their job is broken.

Creating a relevant Service Catalog

So, what does an IT manager do to develop an effective Service Catalog? The answer is twofold. First, it is important to recognize that the Business Unit customers of IT don't want to review detailed catalogs in 'IT-speak'. This challenge is compounded by the fact that most Service Catalog templates are rooted in the IT community's technical roots. The common tendency is to focus on the underlying technical infrastructure and support activities performed by IT, but not on how the service will be interpreted and acted upon by its customers.

The technical details of a service may matter to IT – and perhaps they should matter to the customers of IT – but the simple fact is that the employees and executives in the Business Units won't understand the service unless the description is written in terms they can understand. The customers of IT are too busy to be bothered about whether the email system's SLA is 99.999% or 99.98% up-time, or whether the Help Desk average call-wait time is 30 seconds or 60 seconds. They just want email to work and someone to answer the phone when they call.

Service Catalog documents, written in techno-speak, never achieve the expected results because they never connect with the customer and their business concerns. They may provide extensive and exhaustive service documentation, yet they fail to articulate those services in a way that is meaningful to the business. Ultimately, the majority of such Service Catalog documents are rarely seen or read by the End User and Business Unit community – and thus have little to no impact. IT then continues to do what it has always been doing, and the customers of IT continue to complain that IT is too costly and not responsive to their concerns.

To be effective, the Service Catalog must be relevant to the customer, written in a way that can be understood by any End User or Business Unit executive, easily accessible from a web browser, and flexible to accommodate changes to the business. In order to build an actionable Service Catalog, it must contain services in terms that are familiar and can be easily understood by the customer. In other words, a Service Catalog cannot be simply a list of what the IT organization thinks it does, nor a collection of related IT System component or CIs.

The most common mistake IT organizations make is to articulate their services from an IT perspective – from the CMDB out. Instead, the services contained in a customer-friendly Service Catalog must be written in non-technical terminology and address an immediate concern or need of the customer. If possible, each service should tie to a desired business goal or outcome. For example, customers of IT may want to increase the size limit on their email inbox or create a new distribution list. But they don't necessarily care about the technical specifics of the email system or the number of email servers that IT needs to satisfy these and other demands.

Successful Service Catalogs are defined from the customer in, rather than from the infrastructure out. When endeavoring to create a Service Catalog that speaks in a language familiar to the customer, turn for guidance to real-life catalogs that customers use every day. Internal customers include the employees, Business Unit executives, and even other IT managers throughout the company. They are all consumers, and in today's world, they are intimately familiar with the online sites of companies such as Amazon.com and eBay. These familiar websites process thousands of transactions every day from your internal customers – this is the type of catalog that they expect to interact with and use from their IT Service providers.

To be rapidly adopted and continuously used, the catalog must look like these online consumer catalogs, with easy-to-understand descriptions and an intuitive storefront interface for browsing available Service Offerings. Effective Service Catalogs should also segment the customers they serve – whether End Users, Business Unit executives or other IT managers – and provide different content based on role and needs. When one segments Business Customers from End Users, or vice-versa, one begins to think differently about the construction of and definition of a Service Catalog.

Both Business Customers and End Users of IT Services expect an Amazon.com-styled experience when they are making a Service Request from IT. Business customers have additional expectations from a Service Catalog, however, which are most often focused around budgeting and planning concerns. The bad news is that in this context the catalog metaphors that can be found at Amazon.com online no longer fully apply. The good news is that there is an equally rich source upon which to draw: the marketing brochures and catalogs of the managed service providers, which for the most part are available on their websites. The Service Catalog should therefore draw upon the way IT retailers and IT managed service providers are conditioning customers (End Users and Business Customers alike) to think about and interact with IT Services. As a starting point, this means that the IT Service Catalog should contain the elements listed in table 5.1 – all of which customers have come to expect and demand from their other catalog-based providers.

Key Objectives	Catalog Elements
Appropriate expectations	Service names, descriptions
Service level commitments	Pricing, SLA metrics
Efficient searching	Categories, keywords, icons
Streamlined ordering	Auto-fill forms
Complete orders	Service-specific forms
Correct orders	Field-level instructions
Real-time status	Status e-mail templates

Table 5.1 Service Catalog elements

In addition to being written in language that is familiar to the customer and relevant to their business concerns, an effective Service Catalog needs to meet customers where they are. This means it needs to be transactional in nature.

Creating a transactional Service Catalog
A consumer viewing an online catalog at Amazon.com assumes that if he/she sees something in the catalog that it can be ordered. The same must hold true for a Service Catalog from IT. If the Service Catalog does not also provide the means by which services are requested and fulfilled, then it will not be viewed or used.

IT matters to End Users when something is broken or when they need to request something. IT matters to Business Unit customers when they are building their budgets or when they receive the bill. It is at these moments that the Service Catalog needs to be available and actionable.

To be effective, the Service Catalog must be the means by which services are offered and business is transacted – readily accessible at the moment customers want to transact business – or it simply won't be read or used. Successful Service Catalogs support service ordering, with an electronic shopping cart approach to submitting Service Requests and tracking services online, and provide a link to service consumption and billing/budgeting.

This means that the published service offerings must be tied to service delivery operations, with a Service Catalog that contains the elements listed in the table 5.2.

■ 5.3 The governing nature of the Service Catalog

As should be obvious by now, we do not see the Service Catalog as simply a written document, but rather as a key enabler of various front-office and back-office processes. In the balance of this section we will examine the relationship between the Service Catalog and the development and maturation of the various processes and practices that IT organizations are striving to put in place in order to run more like a business.

Key Objectives	Catalog Elements
Organizational design	Service teams, work queues
Governance	Standard authorizations
Consistency	Standard delivery plans
Quality	Checklists
Efficiency and speed	Intelligent workflows
Automation	Task-level APIs
Appropriate expectations	Service level standards
Continuous improvement	Operating level standards
Control	Alerts and escalations

Table 5.2 Service Catalog elements

Key among these are ITIL's Service Support and Service Delivery processes, with particular emphasis on Change and Configuration Management. As the importance, business criticality, complexity and interdependence of systems and devices that IT provides and supports grows, it is becoming imperative that IT develops mature, cross-functional processes for tracking and managing infrastructure changes, so that critical systems and devices don't fail. In this context we see the Service Catalog and the CMDB as something like two sides of the same coin, bound together by the SLM and Change processes.

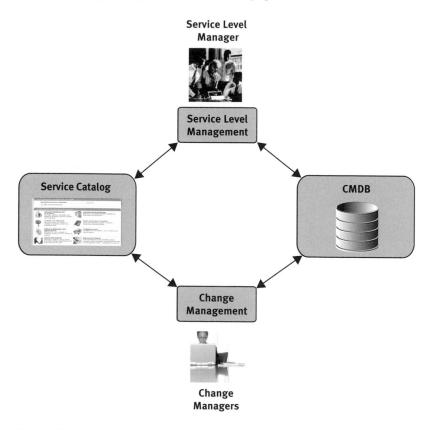

Figure 5.1 The Service Catalog and the CMDB bound together by the SLM and Change processes

Service Catalogs and the SLM Process

The Service Offerings and IT Services defined and managed in the Service Catalog provide the structure in which IT Systems and CIs housed in the CMDB can be understood from a business perspective. Essentially, the Service Catalog becomes the face of IT to the Business Customer, the communication vehicle for articulating and negotiating appropriate Service Offerings and terms, and the source of record for the organization's service structure. In parallel the CMDB becomes the source of record for the physical instances of CIs and IT Systems that are deployed in support of subscribed-to Service Offerings. SLM's role includes the bridging of these two systems so that each can be optimized to perform its independent roles, while staying in synch at the macro level so that they can speak to and inform each other.

An example of the relationship that exists between the Service Catalog, SLM and the CMDB might be something like the following. A Business Customer subscribes to the Service Offering called Business Intelligence, which itself includes IT Services (e.g. Custom Report Writing) that have no relation to IT Systems, as well as IT Services (e.g. hosting of a Business Intelligence Application) that are intimately connected to IT Domains (Servers, Databases, etc.). As part of the overall Service Offering there may be included cost and service level objectives that are dependent on, perhaps, usage and availability of certain Configuration Items connected to the relevant IT Systems. The Service Level Manager would want to look to the CMDB to provide actual usage and performance data as they are consolidating billing and performance data for presentation back to the Business Customer.

It is important to note that not all of the data needed by the Service Level Manager and/or Relationship Manager for his or her interactions with the Business Customer will be contained in the CMDB, since some of the likely relevant cost drivers and service level objectives would not be related to CIs contained in the CMDB. In the example just given this would be the case, for example, with respect to the cost and service levels associated with the included IT Service called Custom Report Building, which would typically be billed on a time-and-materials basis.

Service Catalogs and Change Management Processes

Change Management is the process by which the provisioning of or changes to Configuration Items are managed. Service within the Service Catalog which can be requested or ordered by End Users (i.e. Service Requests) may trigger tasks to provision and/or change Configuration Items controlled by the Change and Configuration processes.

An awareness within the Service Catalog of what Service Requests should trigger formal Change processes enables a Change and Configuration manager to embed business rules in the catalog that automatically trigger Change tickets and thereby drive compliance to stated Change processes. Similarly, an awareness within the Service Catalog of which of these triggered changes can be considered Standard Requests for Change, enables the Service Catalog to push these types of changes through a more cost-effective and efficient self-service and automated provisioning model, while maintaining the integrity of the Change and Configuration Management processes.

Figure 5.2 illustrates how a Service Catalog can act as a 'single pane of glass' by which various classes of requests are initiated, which in turn triggers different Service Support processes, all of which remains transparent and seamless to the End User.

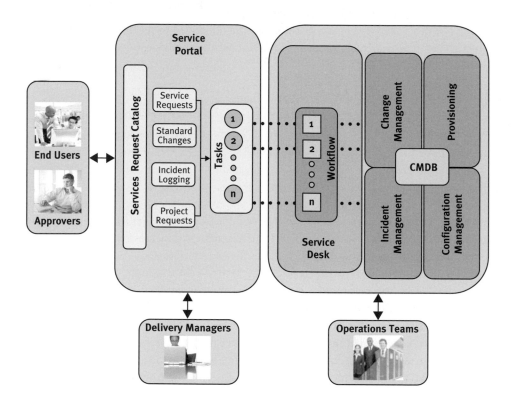

Figure 5.2 The Service Catalog can act as a 'single pane of glass'

■ 5.4 Beyond ITIL Service Support: The Business Perspective

Today, the primary means by which IT interacts with its customers as an organization is via the Service Desk. Beyond the Incidents and Service Requests initiated through the Service Desk, however, a larger percentage of the interaction and coordination among and between Business Customers, End Users and the various IT delivery teams is conducted on an ad-hoc basis via meetings, emails, spreadsheets and phone calls. The typical scenario is depicted in figure 5.3.

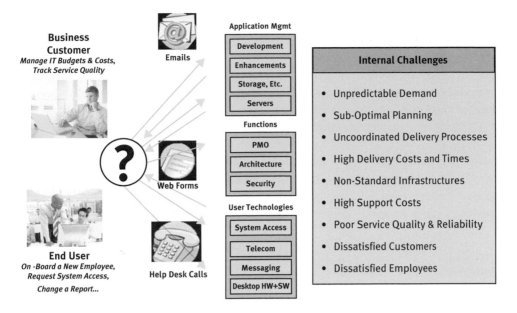

Figure 5.3 Interaction between Business Customers, End Users and the various IT delivery teams

As discussed in previous sections, an effective Service Catalog is actionable in the sense that it is both relevant to Business Customers and End Users, and provides the mechanism for interacting with and coordinating with IT.

For the End User this means the ability to log onto a website and see all of the services available to him or her from the IT organization (and potentially other organizations), and the ability to easily search for and find what is relevant and available to them. Then, once a relevant Service is found the End User should be able to press an order button to request it. They should be able to do this without having to understand how that Service is assembled, nor how the various delivery silos need to coordinate to deliver it. Too often in many IT organizations the End User bears the burden of service assembly and service delivery coordination (i.e. the equivalent of wanting a car, but having to buy and assemble it from its parts).

Basically, what End Users desire is a simple Amazon.com-styled catalog that gives them access to IT. Over the past several years we have worked with a number of companies to implement Service Catalogs that quickly became the number one most-visited site on their company's corporate intranet. They were able to do this by providing a catalog of available services that were both understandable and orderable. The simple message here is "if you build it they will come". The sub-text is that if is not built, they may very well end up going somewhere else. This kind of functionality is becoming a basic expectation for how products and services are provided both external to, and within, corporations.

For the Business Customer who pays the provisioning and support bill for all of the hardware, software, storage and labor requested and consumed by the End User, the expectations of how they should interact with IT are not as well established. In conversations with numerous companies over the past several years one thing, however, has become clear: above all else Business Customers want and are demanding more visibility into and control over how their IT budget dollars are being spent. They want knobs and levers to be able to plan the allocation of scarce resources, and control the spending of their organizations. In essence what they are asking for is a Portfolio of their IT Services that they can use to define and plan an investment mix that is appropriate for their current business realities.

Effective Service Catalogs provide a Business Customer just such a 'portfolio view' including the means by which IT Relationship Managers can work with Business Customers to optimize what Services are provided, agree upon cost and quality trade-offs, forecast demand and, ultimately, track and communicate actual consumption, costs and performance.

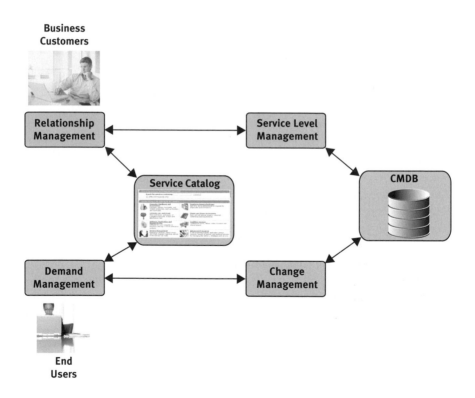

Figure 5.4 The Service Catalog as a bridge between IT silos and their End Users and Business Customers

Figure 5.4 depicts how an effective Service Catalog can bridge the gap and disconnect between IT technical and functional silos and their End Users and Business Customers. By putting in place basic customer relationship management processes, such as Demand Management and Portfolio Management, the IT organization truly begins to function as an integrated business would.

Building the front office of IT

Once an IT organization puts in place an actionable Service Catalog in support of its basic customer relationship processes, it can then turn its attention to defining and optimizing the core 'front-office' processes it needs to run as a business. Vendor Management, Financial Management, Service Delivery and Service Lifecycle Management processes can be honed and optimized to support the efficient delivery of IT Services.

We call these processes 'front office' processes so as not to confuse them with the 'back office' processes described by ITIL Service Support and Service Delivery. Incident, Change, Availability, Capacity and so on are processes that are in many ways unique to IT and necessary for IT to function effectively as an integrated organization, but they are not processes one would typically associate with customer management or running a business.

Figure 5.5 depicts the core front-office process, the roles these processes support, their relationship to the Service Catalog and the core ITIL Service Support and Service Delivery processes.

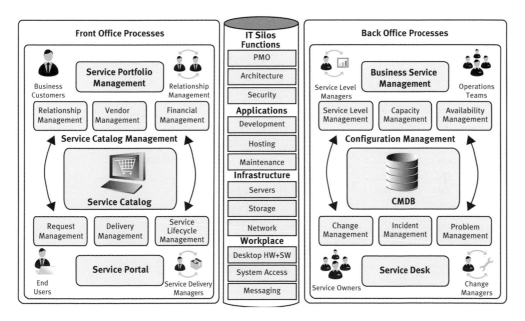

Figure 5.5 Front-office processes and roles, their relationship to the Service Catalog and the core ITIL processes

■ 5.5 Delivering business value

By this point in the book it should be clear that the opportunities and challenges for IT organizations, as they embark upon a journey to run more like a business, are quite large. The implication, of course, is that it will take time, effort, system support and ultimately money and executive backing to succeed. Clearly, a business case will need to be built for the Service Catalog project.

In the final section of this chapter, to assist as the business case is built and to focus efforts, we identify and detail the business successes achieved by companies we have worked with over recent years on Service Catalog and Service Management initiatives. Before we jump into the details of each company's business justifications and results, it is worth pointing out that across all successful initiatives we tend to find evidence of the following two traits:

1. A foundation of quick wins: Successful large-scale projects tend to succeed based upon the success of a relatively modest first phase that can prove the concept, produce meaningful results, and prove the capability of the project team. Based on early success, momentum builds and projects begin to drive themselves toward success.

2. A focus on business value: Successful project teams are generally zealots about articulating and communicating the business value that their projects are delivering.

Defining your starting point

One thing that is common across all the companies we worked with as they made the transition to an IT organization running more like a business, is that in one form or another they started by defining who their customers were and the services they provided to those customers – in other words they started with the definition and creation of a Service Catalog. Within this general strategy, however, there are two starting points that we have seen to be effective. In broad terms companies tend to follow either a 'top down' or 'bottom up' strategy to the definition of their Service Catalog.

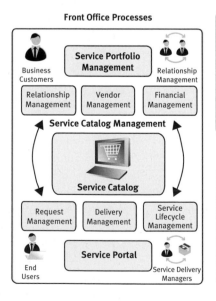

The Top Down Approach

- Start with rationalization of IT services and organization

- Focus on alignment with the Business, improve visibility into IT

- Expand in subsequent steps to day-to-day service activities

The Bottom Up Approach

- Start with rationalization of service request and delivery processes

- Focus on the End User experience

- Expand in subsequent steps to broader organizational change

Figure 5.6 A 'top down' or 'bottom up' strategy

Top-down implementation strategies

The 'top down' strategy is most closely aligned with the ITIL's SLM process, in that it is orientated around the concerns of IT's Business Customer and tends to have a heavy orientation towards the definition of already-deployed applications and application environments as IT Services. Companies that adopt this strategy tend to be most concerned about changing the value-exchange conversation between IT and the Business Customer.

The benefits of this strategy are that it follows the tried and true advice to "follow the money". It focuses initially on the heart of the IT/business alignment challenge. This strategy often has a secondary benefit in that the definition of IT Services from a top-down perspective can give orientation to a related Configuration Management/CMDB initiative, which might otherwise struggle to develop a CMDB structure orientated to support the needs of the Service Level Manager, Relationship Manager and Business Customer.

A challenge associated with a top-down strategy is that it is in many ways the 'big bang' approach to change. As an organization attempts to address the value-exchange conversation with the Business Customer it necessarily impacts the annual budgeting conversation. It also tends to force a level of financial and cost accounting maturity within IT organizations that is often beyond their reach in the early phases of a project.

Bottom-up implementation strategies

A 'bottom up' strategy regarding the definition and development of a Service Catalog as part of broader transformation of IT is more closely aligned with ITIL Service Support processes and functions, such as Change Management and Service Desk, in that the Service Catalog is initially orientated around the day-to-day needs of IT End Users. Companies that adopt this strategy tend to be most concerned about optimizing their Service Request processes and practices as a starting point for broader change.

A benefit of this strategy is that it allows the IT organization to practice organizing itself around relatively simple services (e.g. adding a desktop or managing application access) before tackling the job of articulating deployed-application infrastructures as services. The other benefit is that while a top-down strategy is most often tied to an annual planning or budgeting cycle, meaning that benefits are realized and made visible on a year-to-year pace, a bottom-up strategy can be actualized in parts in less than 90 days in many cases. Also, the Service Catalog becomes something that is accessed and used hundreds of times every day. It quickly becomes the 'new face' of IT, generating real savings and benefits immediately (see discussion on benefits in the next section). Putting this all together, it provides the IT organization with a quick, visible and tangible win that provides clearance, support and experience to drive top-down changes in the future.

Defining your value proposition

At the end of the day where you choose to start is intimately tied to the question of where you are going. What should drive your choice is a clear understanding of the business value that matters most to your organization. In the balance of this section we will examine the various specific value propositions that can be articulated in support of both 'top down' and 'bottom up' strategies.

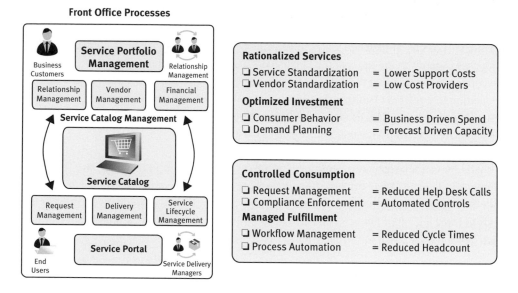

Figure 5.7 Rationalized Services and Controlled Consumption

Based on our experience Service Catalog business cases tend to be organized and focused around one or more of the following themes (see figure 5.7):
1. Rationalizing Services
2. Optimizing Investment
3. Controlling Consumption
4. Managing Fulfillment

Rationalizing Services through the Service Catalog and Portfolio Management
Just the act of taking an inventory of existing services and then documenting those services in the context of business value in the form of a Service Catalog will almost certainly lead to a rationalization of what IT is doing. It will force IT and its Business Customers to ask and answer the question: "Does what we are doing today really make sense going forward?" To borrow a few examples from some of our customers: Does it make sense to have three different applications that calculate Puerto Rican excise tax? Does it make sense to have three different flavors of email supported? Does it make sense to have non-mission-critical applications consume platinum-level storage resources?

The result of this exercise is inevitably the standardization of supported Services around what makes sense from a business perspective. Such standardization can have a dramatic impact on an IT organization's support costs and both the number and complexity of supported Services decreases.

■ **Real-world example:**

One of the world's largest chemical companies generated cost savings of 30% on PCs by migrating from over 14 different desktop platforms to two standard desktop and laptop models.

Table 5.3 provides a simple 'order of magnitude' calculation for determining potential savings as part of your business case for investing in the creation and use of a Service Catalog.

	Conservative	Aggressive
# of unique IT services	100	100
Average TCO per IT service/yr	$500K	$500K
Total IT Service Management spend	$50M	$50M
% standardization opportunity	6%	14%
Total Annual ROI	$3M	$7M

Table 5.3 Service standardization: Reducing overall service and support costs by standardizing and rationalizing services, resulting in systems and process standardization

Once service offerings are rationalized accordingly, the next logical step is to rationalize service providers and source to the low-cost provider. Armed with a list of required Service Offerings, the provider's Service Elements and related service levels and internal costs, one can begin to evaluate whether the internal IT organization is best equipped to deliver the service, or whether a particular service is a candidate for selective outsourcing.

An 'order of magnitude' calculation of savings is represented in table 5.4.

	Conservative	Aggressive
# of unique IT services	100	100
Average TCO per IT service/yr	$500K	$500K
Total IT Service Management spend	$50M	$50M
% strategic sourcing opportunity	6%	11%
Total Annual ROI	$3M	$5.5M

Table 5.4 Vendor standardization: Understand service costs and reduce overall costs by sourcing services with the low cost provider (strategic sourcing)

■ **Key takeaways:**

- There is more value to be attained through an ongoing, structured process of service and vendor rationalization, supported by an 'evergreen' Service Catalog.

Optimizing investment through the Service Catalog and Relationship Management
Today most organizations have squeezed down unit costs about as far as they can go through traditional means – data center consolidation, vendor negotiations and so on. Yet, while they are being asked to cut spending ever more, the demand for IT Services is increasing as the result of expanding user bases, new devices and systems being added to the infrastructure, and new, higher quality standards as IT Services become more and more mission-critical. The result is the real need to do more with less.

With effective relationship management practices and processes, supported by a robust Service Catalog, IT organizations can prepare themselves for what is sometimes referred to as the next frontier of cost-saving opportunities: 'right sizing' demand. Right-sizing demand means introducing demand levers that provide Relationship Managers and Business Customers with the ability to negotiate demand. These kind of levers or controls can be as simple as providing visibility into usage and demand patterns to enable planning conversations, or as complex as pricing controls which allow the business to determine investments.

The challenge today is that most IT organizations lack an understanding of the needs of their customers from a business perspective. Also, Business Customers typically have little visibility into what they are spending on IT and what they are getting in return – weakening IT's relationship with the businesses and fueling the perception of the IT organization as a Cost Center that needs to be squeezed.

In many leading corporations, the relationship management role has proven critical to establishing IT credibility – as the liaison between Business Unit customers and the IT organization. In other companies, it simply becomes the central complaint department because it lacks effective tools and information to manage the business relationship. Establishing and sustaining a meaningful dialog between Business Customers and the IT organization requires a common understanding of available IT Services, with clear definitions that align with business needs; shared criteria for success, with the ability to monitor key operational and business metrics; and a proactive approach to uncovering future service needs based on Business Unit demand.

Nothing will improve IT's standing with the business more than bringing service level 'knobs' and 'dials' to the table which enable Business Customers to rationalize the cost/benefit balance for themselves. By delivering greater transparency and options, the Service Catalog helps Business Customers of IT make appropriate decisions at the budget planning level. For instance, when the Business Customer understands that same-day service costs three times the amount of two-day service, then he or she can decide if their portfolio of available services needs to include the more expensive option.

This kind of dialog enables IT Relationship Managers to create a tailored portfolio of Service Offerings for their Business Customers. Once the IT Relationship Manager and Business Customer agree on the service terms, Service Offerings are converted to Business Agreements which describe the services, expected consumption and promised service levels. The Business Agreements become the basis for measuring and demonstrating the business value delivered by IT. All along, both sides are dealing with concrete, discrete units of Service Offerings that can be examined, compared, understood, assembled and disassembled, effectively killing the negative assessment of IT as a black box.

The following tables provide a simple 'order of magnitude' calculation for determining potential savings as part of your business case for investing in the creation and use of a Service Catalog to support relationship management practices and processes.

	Conservative	Aggressive
# of unique IT services	100	100
Average TCO per IT service/yr	$500K	$500K
Total IT Service Management spend	$50M	$50M
% business driven spend opportunity	5%	10%
Total Annual ROI	$2.5M	$5M

Table 5.5 Consumer behavior: Reduce demand variablitiy, control service level overspending and limit service demand volume growth, by driving spend decisions from the Business

	Conservative	Aggressive
# of unique IT services	100	100
Average TCO per IT service/yr	$500K	$500K
Total IT Service Management spend	$50M	$50M
% 'buffer' resources	5%	5%
% demand planning opportunity	25%	50%
Total Annual ROI	$625K	$1.2M

Table 5.6 Demand planning: Reduce resource buffers through active and accurate demand forecast processes and practices

■ **Key takeaways:**

- Proactive Relationship Management is a key area of potential savings.
- Achieving these savings requires that you implement 'demand levers' through an automated Service Catalog and relationship management tool.

Controlling consumption through the Service Catalog and Demand Management
Most large companies have multiple, conflicting and disparate mechanisms for ordering or requesting internal services – often with hundreds of web forms and several homegrown Service Request applications. End Users can't find what they need, and if they do find the right form, they are often forced to retype the same data again and again. As a result, End Users continue to call the Help Desk or use the 'shoulder tap' method to submit Service Requests.

This creates chaos and confusion for both the End User and the IT Service delivery organization. The burden is on the requestor – or designated 'process shepherds' and coordinators – to navigate through these various ordering mechanisms, determine who does what, manage the various tasks associated with every request, and ensure that the request is fulfilled. In addition the service delivery teams spend an inordinate amount of time responding to requests, researching requirements, validating information and providing status updates.

A single web-based destination for End Users to browse or search for services, order services and monitor delivery status – with an interface personalized to their needs and a catalog of standardized services reflective of their function's position, location and associated permissions – provides a means by which an IT organization can pull End Users to a self-service Service Request model. A familiar shopping cart metaphor – similar to Amazon.com or Dell.com – means no training is required for ordering and tracking services. All together this means eliminating the costly 'middle-man' that is the Service Desk call.

While generating costs savings for IT, the Service Catalog becomes a convenience for End Users. Leveraging a familiar e-commerce metaphor, a Service Catalog can help End Users find the services they need, smooth the ordering process, and clearly set expectations on what will be delivered and when. Be warned, however, that when an End User is looking at an online Service Catalog they won't compare it to other IT shops or best-in-class IT shops. They will compare it to their experiences using other e-commerce sites like Google, Yahoo, Amazon, FedEx and Dell. This is a high standard to meet, but there is software that makes this possible and inexpensive. There are really no excuses for sloppiness in this area.

■ Real-world example:

One of the world's largest telecommunications companies was able to eliminate 40,000 calls a year to the Service Desk and re-allocate 21 'process shepherds' while growing more than 45% through the introduction of an effective self-service request catalog, linked to their back-end fulfillment silos.

Table 5.7 provides a simple 'order of magnitude' calculation for determining potential savings as part of your business case for investing in the creation and use of a Service Catalog that supports self-service request management.

	Conservative	Aggressive
# service requests/yr routed via the Help Desk	40,000	40,000
Average help desk cost/call	$10	$10
Total transaction costs	$400K	$400K
% eliminate via self-service	75%	100%
Total Annual ROI	$300K	$400K

Table 5.7 Request management: Reducing service request costs through the use of a self-service, actionable service catalog

Once an organization has its End Users trained to go to one place to initiate Service Requests – a 'request center' of sorts – then the organization can use this convergence of requests to embed and manage key business controls. Order-on-behalf functionality allows managers or administrative contacts to submit Service Requests for other employees in a controlled manner. Approval and authorization business rules can be embedded in the definition of the defined services. Similarly, service-specific business rules can be defined, documented and enforced (e.g. Sarbanes-Oxley related rules regarding access to systems and data).

From a business-case construction perspective, the key is that once you have a Service Catalog defined, you can use it to document and enforce controls that will, in many cases, have the impact of reducing consumption. End Users don't see what they can't get. Managers have a means by which they can moderate consumption on the part of their reports. Simply publishing costs, even if they are not connected to charge-back practices, helps End Users become good consumers and stewards of the organization's money.

Demand-management solutions help at the tactical day-to-day level by presenting to End Users only those services that the Business Unit executive has authorized them to order. That's the first level of control. If a service is not there it is because the business decided it couldn't afford it. IT, then, is not forced to police the End User community. Instead, Service Delivery Managers can focus on shaping demand, not just saying no. Shaping demand becomes an exercise in guiding behavior with a carrot instead of a stick. It is about creating enticing offerings that people will want. Demand is shaped by price, delivery speed, approval structures and usage policies. We have seen that just pricing a service, even without actually charging for it, changes End User behavior and decreases demand by more than 40% in some cases. Just communicating what the company pays helps employees change their own behavior. In other cases we have seen that offering standard models in short and reliable delivery cycles, as opposed to longer and less reliable cycles for non-standard models, drives people to accept the standard.

■ Real-world example:

A global high-technology manufacturing company deployed a Service Catalog in which it published the costs of key services, even though it did not actually charge the End User for services requested. The result was a greater than 50% reduction in the consumption of certain expensive services. The Service Catalog empowered the End Users to be good stewards.

Table 5.8 provides a simple 'order of magnitude' calculation for determining potential savings as part of your business case for investing in the creation and use of a Service Catalog that supports controls designed to influence and moderate demand.

■ Key takeaways:

- Proactive Demand Management is a key area of potential savings.
- Achieving these savings requires you to implement a Service Catalog that provides one-stop shopping for End User Service Requests.

	Conservative	Aggressive
# service requests/yr	50,000	50,000
Average cost to provision	$100	$100
Total Service Delivery costs	$5M	$5M
% eliminated via controls	5%	10%
Total Annual ROI	$250K	$500K

Table 5.8 Compliance enforcement: Reducing service request costs through the use of controls (e.g. approvals, published costs, etc.)

Managing fulfillment through the Service Catalog and Delivery Management

Most IT organizations are organized around technical silos, characterized by their own set of processes, systems and standards. Without a single system for managing the entire end-to-end service delivery process, routing requests across departments is often problematic. Data frequently needs to be re-keyed into different systems, creating added administrative work for service teams and increasing the chance for errors along the way. In addition, because there is often no mechanism for viewing the status of a request across multiple service teams, service orders sometimes get lost in 'black holes' – the entire process needs to start all over again, wasting valuable resources.

An actionable Service Catalog can seamlessly span across disparate IT groups and departments to expedite service fulfillment. Repeatable workflow processes can be standardized, defined as a component of a service definition, and then automated in order to replace redundant and labor-intensive data entry.

■ Real-world example:

A global hotel and resort company included standardized delivery process definitions as part of its Service Catalog, and then automated the link between requested services and back-office work management and provisioning systems. With respect to just one service area (identity and access management) alone, the company was able to re-allocate several process shepherds and reduce typical service delivery cycle times from 5 days to 5 seconds by automating the entire fulfillment and provisioning process.

Table 5.9 and 5.10 provide a simple 'order of magnitude' calculation for determining potential savings as part of your business case for investing in the creation and use of a Service Catalog that includes within its scope related Service Delivery processes and automated links to back-end fulfillment and provisioning systems.

Delivery management ensures that processes to fulfill the End User request run smoothly and cost-effectively. Since End Users are requesting standard offerings, the delivery work plans can also be standardized, and in many cases, fully automated by some IT Systems, to speed delivery and eliminate errors.

	Conservative	Aggressive
# of process shepherds	5	5
Average cost/yr	$100K	$100K
Total spend	$500K	$500K
% reduction w/workflow	75%	100%
Total Annual ROI	$375K	$500K

Table 5.9 Workflow Management: Reducing overall service and support costs by leveraging workflow technology to eliminate "process shepherds"

ITIL covers this type of process under Change Management, but we would like to add two refinements to the ITIL definition. First, a Change Management process is traditionally optimized to prevent negative impacts to delivery of IT services, and thus there are logical controls and stages to the process. A delivery process is optimized for speed, reliability and efficiency. Both are changes, but they have divergent goals.

Second, the Change Management process can be tiered into two or three variations, such as no impact, standard and high risk. Delivery processes will have hundreds of variations. Work plans and workflows will by definition introduce quite a bit of variability. Tools that enable those variations easily are needed to capture the savings available.

	Conservative	Aggressive
# of provisioning personnel	10	10
Average cost/yr	$100K	$100K
Total spend	$1M	$1M
% reduction w/workflow	20%	40%
Total Annual ROI	$200K	$400K

Table 5.10 Process automation: Reducing overall service and support costs by leveraging technology to automate manual provisioning tasks

Key takeaways:

- Integrating Service Request and service delivery is another area of potential savings.
- Achieving these savings requires that you implement a Service Catalog that includes service delivery processes within its scope.

Provide visibility to re-establish credibility

The final value-add is brought by visibility resulting from the combined efforts, described above. With standardized, discrete services, IT can now answer questions about performance and cost that it could not prior to the catalog implementation. Properly tooled catalogs should deliver a lush river of metrics about Service Delivery effectiveness, efficiency and traceability across all constituencies.

- Business unit executives get visibility into the actual versus budget impact of consumption by their End Users. This information can be monitored relative to key business drivers – cost per new employee or cost per order – rather than along just the IT-centric technical measures that most IT reporting systems use.
- IT executives and IT Relationship Managers are proactively notified of delivery bottlenecks or SLA and budget exceptions to allocate resources appropriately. Armed with, in effect, an early-warning radar, Relationship Managers can change the dynamic of interactions with their Business Unit customer from reactive – "I'll fix it when you call" to proactive – "I'll fix it before there is a problem." Being proactive is a key threshold for re-establishing trust and demonstrating to the business that IT adds value at each step of the process.
- End Users can get summary or detailed progress reports on the status of their Service Requests. Automatic alerts and escalations help ensure that End Users are aware of unexpected changes in the fulfillment schedules.
- The service delivery teams are able to assess current and forecasted demand to ensure the right resources are available to deliver work. Reports and analytics on utilization, quality and rework levels allow service delivery teams to remain agile in the face of changing business requirements.

Promising results

A recent case study we conducted of 191 End Users in large corporations showed that customers who used Service Catalogs as their primary way of ordering from IT reported they were 'Very Satisfied' or 'Extremely Satisfied' with the value delivered by IT 63% of the time, compared to just 41% for users who did not have access to a Service Catalog – a 22% difference. The difference in End User satisfaction can mean the difference between an IT organization that fights quarter after quarter for budget, and one that is able to earn the trust of its customers to find new and innovative ways to bring profit to the bottom line.

Putting it all together

Not every Service Catalog will address all of the potential opportunities highlighted in this section. Most successful initiatives start by focusing on one area of potential savings and optimize their project to deliver results before moving on to other areas.

Regardless of where you choose to focus, the key message of this section is that your Service Catalog initiative can and should be designed to produce real, tangible business results for your organization.

A Step-by-step Approach to IT Success

An actionable Service Catalog, as should be obvious by now, can be the foundation for transforming an IT organization from a loosely federated bunch of technical and functional silos into an integrated organization that functions as a business would, with customers, products, supply chains, vendors and financial management. What we are talking about, then, is a major transformational initiative that can seem rather daunting.

The purpose of this section is to help guide you through this transformational process. Based on our experiences over the past several years at all stages of this journey, we have attempted to articulate here a path to success. While each starting point and journey will be unique, we believe the following to be the six most common and important steps to running an IT organization like a business (in the order we think they should be performed, see figure 6.1).

Step 1: Treat users like customers

To improve the alignment between services offered and employee needs, the service organization must treat its internal customer as if they were a traditional external revenue-generating customer. By approaching the employee like a customer, the mind-set of the organization shifts to identify and address customer needs first and foremost.

Step 2: Standardize and catalog best practices

Another fundamental shift in the approach service organizations must make is to re-examine all the individual processes used to deliver a given service. To build a service-oriented culture, the service organization must view its services offerings like 'products'. Similar to proven manufacturing methods, where physical goods are produced the same way each time, services should be delivered using identifiable and repeatable processes.

Step 3: Implement SLAs

One of the most common sources of customer dissatisfaction with service delivery teams is miscommunication – and in many cases no communication – around when services will actually be delivered and with what level of quality. By implementing SLAs, the customer and the service delivery team have a common understanding of how long a service should take to be completed and the level of performance to be expected from the service. SLAs provide a known benchmark that service delivery teams and customers can use to measure the responsiveness of the service delivery.

Step 4: Start pricing and charge-backs for services

Customers who are not charged for internal services often perceive the value as commensurate with what they pay. When the customer pays nothing for a service, the perspective is that the service received is without value and internal services come without cost. And without a price, demand for services is virtually unconstrained. This is why best-in-class service delivery organizations set a competitive price and either charge for the services delivered, or publish the price even if no active charge-back system is in place, for the purpose of inducing typical consumer behavior.

Step 5: Evaluate strategic (selective) outsourcing

Many global organizations outsource one or more service delivery functions today. For many types of services, outsourcers can provide a cost-effective alternative to internal service delivery. But repeated research studies show that wholesale outsourcing of complete business processes often delivers less than expected results. Service delivery thought-leaders recommend an ongoing process where internal service delivery is compared to outsourced alternatives on a task-by-task basis. The key is to find areas where others can perform a function more effectively than an internal team and let them do it, while at the same time maintaining control over the basic front and back-office processes of IT.

Step 6: Report, monitor and refine

It is important for the service organization to continually improve upon the processes it has in place. This is both to remain competitive with outside vendors as well as to enhance the service organization's productivity. The service team must leverage process improvement and formal measurement programs to maximize its reliability, effectiveness and efficiency. Currently most companies do not measure the operational effectiveness of their service groups. Because of this, the organization is left without the ability to make positive adjustments to the operational structure.

Companies that begin to run services like a business soon discover that by automating all aspects of the operation, key metrics are automatically captured. Every transaction is logged and tracked on a step-by-step basis because of the very nature of the ordering and fulfillment process. This helps to benchmark service delivery and quantify the time it takes to complete each task. By reviewing the frequency of demand for a given service and the time it takes to fulfill each order, for example, the organization is able to constantly refine its operation to deliver the best possible level of service to its customers.

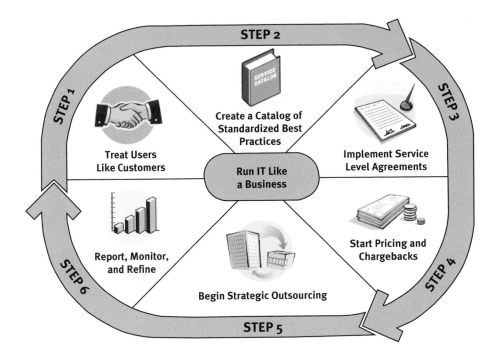

Figure 6.1 A step-by-step approach to IT success

■ 6.1 Step 1: Treat users like customers

A common misperception among companies transitioning to a 'service-delivery-as-a-business' model is that the change is simply mechanical, such as the manner in which service teams are organized. Moving forward without changing this perception is a huge mistake.

The first step requires a fundamental shift in the mind-set of the service delivery team. Service delivery is no longer an employee-to-employee or peer-to-peer relationship. What is needed is a shift to a business-to-customer relationship where the service team continually sells the value of the services offered, and the customer's expectations are not only correctly set, but consistently met.

Gone are the days when the internal service delivery team owned a monopoly on service delivery. Now, the customer gets to decide if the quality and value of each service transaction gives the service team the right to bid on the next transaction. Today's customers view the service delivery team like any other vendor – a poorly executed service transaction today can mean the customer shifts to another vendor for tomorrow's Service Request.

For many service organizations, this requires a simple shift in emphasis from how they operate today. For those service organizations that for a long time interacted with internal customers as peers – or in some cases even adversaries – this change can be particularly challenging.

Identify Executive Sponsors

Running services like a business requires a widespread cultural shift within the entire organization. The biggest predictor of success is the existence of an involved and committed executive sponsor. The executive sponsor should be the individual who is the ultimate owner of the overall service operation. In a large organization, that person is sometimes the COO, CIO or VP Shared Services. Regardless of the title, the executive sponsor must be someone who has enough seniority to influence every aspect of the service organization yet maintain a sharp focus on the customer's requirements.

■ **Requirements checklist:**
❏ Prepare for cultural shift
❏ Identify Executive Sponsor

The sponsor should have a very tangible, vested interest in the success of the operation: often an executive sponsor's annual bonus can be tied to whether or not the service organization achieves certain milestones. The primary responsibility of the executive sponsor in this case is to develop a strategy and process that enables the delivery of services to internal customers in the most efficient manner possible. When the executive sponsor fails to take an active role in the re-design of the service organization – or, worse yet, when no executive sponsor has been assigned to the project – the likelihood for success is severely diminished.

Executive Sponsor must be customer-focused

An executive sponsor's first job is to accelerate the service organization's new 'customer-focused' mentality by carefully selecting its initial target set of customers and Service Offerings. The key is to create an open dialog between this customer and the service team, with a focus on what each party can do to resolve problems.

■ **Path-to-success recommendation:**
Start with a small sub-set of internal customers or departments. At the top of the list, consider the customer or department that has been the most vocal about the shortcomings of the service group.

By partnering with your end-user customer for the initial services deployment the customer becomes immersed in the problem/solution discussion. This helps the customer take on a sense of responsibility – or even pride – in the eventual outcome of the project. When the project is completed successfully, the internal customer becomes the poster child and chief spokesperson for the remodeled service organization. Ideally this reference customer becomes an 'evangelist', someone who can offer valuable testimony about the savings or process improvements they have realized. This personal endorsement is vital to the service group's ability to market itself to other internal customers.

Establish new role: Service Level Manager (aka Relationship Manager)

A new role emerges in the service organization with a strong customer focus: the Service Level Manager or Customer Relationship Manager. Similar to an Account Executive at an outside supplier, the Customer Relationship Manager is responsible for interacting with the client groups and advocating customer needs within the service organization. This individual is responsible for ensuring the services offered meet those needs, and they take responsibility for improving processes that negatively affect customer satisfaction.

■ **Requirements checklist:**
- ❑ Assign an Account Executive/Customer Relationship Manager role
- ❑ Understand the customer's key business drivers and ensure service delivery processes and metrics align with those business processes

The role of the Customer Relationship Manager is not simply an administrative one. Rather, this individual must be fully authorized to make important decisions that directly impact the way in which the service chain operates.

The Customer Relationship Manager must be an adept negotiator and sales person. This role is responsible for setting prices and negotiating SLAs for internal services. They also are charged with identifying opportunities in which an outsourced solution best serves the customer's needs.

Share the customer's perspective on appropriate metrics

The Customer Relationship Manager must share the customer's perspective on the metrics the customer already has in place to measure success. The service organization owns the responsibility to draw the operational links between those metrics and the measurements it uses internally.

■ **Path-to-success recommendation:**
Ask each internal customer unit for their 'wish-list' of services and how those services map to the customer's business objectives. This list will help the service organization understand the daily challenges customers face in conducting their business.

By gaining a detailed understanding and greater sensitivity toward the specific business goals of its customers, the service organization can take into account key success and risk factors, as well as the delivery and cost expectations of the customer.

The result should be a relationship in which the service organization adapts its offerings to facilitate the success of each Business Unit in the company. Essentially, the service organization must seek to achieve the golden rule of service delivery: to treat internal customers the same way the service organization expects to be treated by its own vendors.

■ 6.2 Step 2: Standardize and catalog best practices

To move toward a customer-focused strategy, the service delivery group must first have a firm grasp of the services it already provides and how they are being delivered, including the roles and responsibilities of the work teams. This starts with an inventory of people, processes, tools and vendors:

Category	Sample Inventory Considerations
People	• Who can request services? • What are approval and authorization levels? • Who delivers services? Insiders? External service providers?
Processes	• What are the ways services are requested? • Can the same service be requested multiple ways? • How are ad-hoc services handled?
Services	• Are there any 'standard' services? • Is there a catalog or list of services? • What are the top-20 most requested services?
Tools	• What automation is used to track service delivery? • Are there other systems the service delivery tools need to integrate with?
Vendors	• What services does each vendor provide? • What price / performance metrics exist on vendor performance? • What unique skills or advantages does each vendor bring to service delivery?

Table 6.1 Inventory of current people, processes and tools

Furthermore, the service organization needs visibility into the frequency with which each service is requested and/or used across the enterprise. For example, the IT department might learn through investigation that a request to reset an existing network password is submitted at least 10 times as often as a request to create an entirely new password. This information will help guide the creation of new types of password offerings, and identify the areas in which to focus initial automation efforts. Similarly, among the numerous applications an IT organization may support, only a small percentage of these applications are truly mission-critical (an easy starting point may be, for example, applications governed under SOX provisions).

■ Requirements checklist:

❑ Create an inventory of your current processes to identify key people, processes, services, tools and vendors
❑ Identify the most requested/used, high-impact services and start there

Additionally, if possible, the service organization should ask its internal customers to quantify the 'value' each service delivers. This will help the service team identify those services that are critical to meeting the user's business needs, and those that are simply 'nice-to-have' or commodity services.

Unlike traditional enterprise change initiatives that require significant process re-engineering before they can begin to generate a positive ROI, implementing a Service Catalog project can start with "paving the cow path." Many thought-leading organizations simply catalog processes as they are delivered today, and find ways to improve those processes incrementally as they go forward.

Use the inventory to understand what drives demand, cost and value

Through a variety of methods, including customer interviews and review of reports from service delivery systems, you should be able to quickly identify those processes that are:
- Most frequently ordered or used;
- Usually delivered later than expected or at unacceptable levels of service;
- Have the greatest impact on customer and business productivity.

Regardless of the total number of services offered, it is not unusual to see that just the top 25% of services make up nearly 75% of the volume of Service Requests (table 6.2). By focusing the re-engineering effort on those key services, the service delivery team can achieve quick financial and political wins.

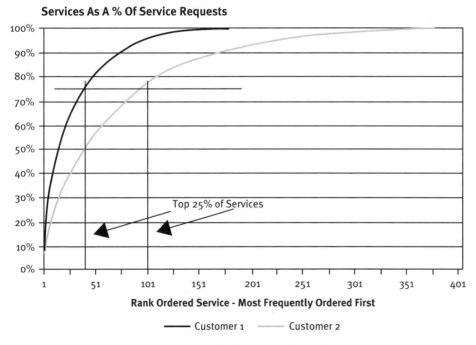

Figure 6.2 The top 25% of services make up nearly 75% of the volume of Service Request

Finally, the service organization must carefully review the descriptions provided for each of the available services. The goal here is to determine whether the descriptions sufficiently articulate the scope of the services, the value provided by the services, and whether the customer has enough information to select the service most suited to their business requirements.

The services inventory and audit helps establish the baseline that should be used to ensure that service delivery improvements generate incremental value.

Path-to-success recommendation:
Balance 'value delivered to customer' with the cost of delivering services to identify the services most in need of improvement. By maintaining a laser-focus on improving the value delivered to customers, the service team earns the credibility to make the incremental investments required to reduce overall cost.

Standardize practices

It is not unusual during this initial service organization audit and documentation process to discover that the same service is delivered differently each time. In fact, most companies have three or more different processes for the same service across geographies, divisions, or even across different individuals to deliver what should be the same service. No wonder customers feel like service delivery is inconsistent.

Virtually every organization discovers that it can consolidate some service offerings to eliminate redundancies and standardize practices across the service chain.

Rather than having one set of process steps to grant network and email access in Detroit, and different steps to grant network and email access in San Francisco, can the same basic set of steps be consolidated into one consistent process? There can be legitimate business reasons why the service processes need to be different, but "we've always done it this way" is not usually one of them.

Requirements checklist:
❑ Force standardization wherever possible to maximize effectiveness
❑ Identify common 'atomic units' of services and create complex services by assembling standard parts

The organization must also identify 'atomic units' that overlap multiple services. For example, a Service Request such as installing a new telephone is likely to be a sub-service for adding a new employee. By standardizing the practice of installing a telephone, the service organization gains visibility into how that specific task fits into more complex Service Requests. This allows the service chain to force a collapse among similar but slightly different services, thus eliminating duplicate delivery teams and redundant steps. Similarly, storage profile for mission-critical applications should be standardized across the enterprise, which in turn brings the ability to optimize vendor contracts and support processes.

Additionally, as the service organization evolves into a customer-focused group, the opportunity to identify bottlenecks and implement solutions becomes apparent. The result is higher quality, faster service delivery and more efficient operation of the entire service chain.

Benchmark against external vendors and similar organizations

The service organization should compare its own offerings against the alternatives, such as competing internal groups and external service providers. There is an abundance of measurement materials available, including industry benchmarks set by business consultants and analyst firms. The service delivery team should keep a careful eye on these metrics when standardizing practices to achieve optimal operational efficiency.

Finally, it is important for the service organization to test the relevance of its offerings with the internal customer prior to enterprise-wide deployment. If the service offerings do not adequately map to the customer's needs, further refinement is necessary.

■ Path-to-success recommendation:

Use service definitions from external providers as templates for defining internal offerings. This makes benchmarking in the future much easier and less expensive.

Create a catalog of Service Offerings

Service catalogs are the heart of any effective service delivery process. A Service Catalog can be a simple list in a Word or Excel document, or as comprehensive as installing specific tools designed to create formal Service Catalogs. The catalog should contain items that are visible to the customer, and additional information that is used by the service delivery team to ensure smooth delivery.

Items visible to the customer include:
• A description of the service;
• Disclosure of any prerequisites or required services;
• Approval levels.

A description of the service

Ideally this description should be in business terms the customer understands. Rather than offering "POP 3 email protocol support with 30MB redundant storage and SLL support", the catalog should offer "email account with secure Internet access from anywhere on the web, including sufficient storage for most light- to medium-users."

Just like a typical retail catalog, the Service Catalog is the opportunity for the service delivery team to market, promote and 'sell' the value they deliver. The best catalog systems support graphics for improved presentation, with logical Yahoo-like categorization of services to make it easy to use and find services. The systems should also support keyword and full-text search of the catalogs to help users find specific services quickly.

Customers are used to making rational decisions such as trading off speed and capabilities for cost. If the catalog presents a choice between good, better and best levels of service and the associated cost differences, then customers can make the selections that are most appropriate for their business needs.

Disclosure of any prerequisites or required services

If the customer needs to ensure there is a second phone line before the fax machine can be installed, the catalog is the optimal place to describe this requirement. This eliminates wasted trips, confusion and frustration. If the prerequisite items can be easily ordered from the catalog, the service team is able to maximize the value it delivers.

Approval levels

Let the customer know what approvals are required for each service. While some services are entitlements – meaning they require no approvals – many services require a manager or higher-level executive to approve the service delivery. Even though many SDM systems manage the approval process automatically, service teams often discover the slowest part of delivering services is getting the appropriate approvals from the employee's management.

Additional information that should be contained in the catalog, but not shown to the customer, includes:
- Operational checklists;
- Details of skill requirements necessary to perform a given Service Request;
- Repeatable delivery methods;
- Escalations;
- Service delivery costs (as distinct from the price that the customer sees).

Organize into logical groupings

The first iteration of the Service Catalog will change as customer activity data and direct feedback are gathered. As such, the Service Catalog must be flexible enough to allow the Product Manager to easily design, create and catalog new services as necessary.

The dynamic nature of Service Catalogs highlights the importance of cataloging, ordering and delivery systems that are tightly integrated and flexible. The total cost of ownership for catalog systems that require programming skills to maintain are significantly higher than those systems that can be maintained by service delivery experts using a non-programmatic interface. Also, if the catalog is integrated with the work-order management system, service delivery costs can be reduced even further.

When the service organization develops the Service Catalog, it should look outside as much as possible to mimic the best practices of others. Commercially available best-practice catalogs include key service delivery tasks common across IT, facilities, telecommunications, workplace services and catalogs that support the best practices.

Service delivery organizations may also find it useful to compare their catalogs to the offerings of external service providers that offer similar types of services. By structuring the Service Catalog in this way, the internal services organization can easily identify which of its offerings are competitive with outside providers.

■ 6.3 Step 3: Implement SLAs

SLAs are critical to establishing and communicating clear expectations about service delivery timeframes and quality. Without clear SLAs, service delivery teams are constantly fighting customer perceptions that service delivery is slow and inconsistent, and that quality of performance is inadequate.

Understand the customer's business

Aligning the service team's offerings with the customer's business objectives is vital to improving the perception and performance of the service team. Unfortunately, service organizations tend to measure success with very different metrics from those used by the internal customers. In many cases, the service organization is so far removed from its customers that it is unfamiliar with the relevant business metrics of the customers they serve, and vice versa.

For example, many IT departments focus on providing five-nines (99.999) percentage up-time and average 2-second response times while their customers are focused on closing a particular sale before the end of a quarter. While the telecommunications team is focused on the logistics surrounding installing a network connection at a trade show, the marketing department executive is concerned about leads getting distributed real-time from the show floor to the field sales person.

The service organization must know its own strengths and weaknesses, and constantly compare them with the changing needs of its customers. Together with the Relationship Manager, the service organization must establish a dialog with every customer to ascertain their business needs and map those against the services that can be requested (see Table 6.2 as an example).

Department Requesting Services	Sample metrics
Sales	• Time to set up home office for new sales rep • Timely and seamless logistics at the customer corporate visit center
Finance	• Timeframe to design and deploy new reports • Accuracy of asset inventory
Engineering	• Ability of CAD medelling systems to handle peak demands • Compliance with security access audits
Human Resourses	• Accuracy and completeness of employee on-board process • Employee workspace complete and functional when employees start

Table 6.2 Examples of business-relevant metrics

Taking the lead from external service providers, today's internal service delivery thought-leaders implement SLAs that measure value-based and operational metrics such as business impact, cost reduction, improved flexibility and risk mitigation – rather than simply availability and response time.

SLAs help manage customer expectations

Fundamentally, SLAs set and manage customer expectations – they are contracts between the service organization and the customer that outline the parameters within which any given requested service will be fulfilled. Customer satisfaction is based upon whether the expectations set out in the SLA are met, exceeded or missed.

■ **Path-to-success recommendation:**

SLAs must be:

- Observable

- Measurable

- Actionable

The SLA should be a living agreement that helps to guide the service organization in continuous process improvement.

Real-world example:

One leading international retailer sets two SLA objectives – an external customer-facing objective and a second, more difficult to achieve internal objective. The service team is managed to continually improve. When compliance rates against the more rigorous internal objective hits 80% to 90%, the service team adjusts the external SLA downward to the new goal, and simultaneously sets the internal objective even higher. Through this process, the service team makes ongoing improvements while still setting customer expectations they can meet. The result is that some processes which initially took 2-3 weeks to complete now take 4-5 days. And the improvement process is continuous – now the team's management expects to reduce that figure even further to 3-4 days in a matter of months.

What should be included in the SLA

Within the SLA itself are details the customer traditionally needs to understand when requesting a service:

• What will it cost?

• How long will it take and how well will it perform when I get it?

Yet these two data points are incomplete for the next generation of service providers. Companies that are migrating toward running services like a business must rely on implementing SLAs that focus on customers and demonstrated business value, not just cost and timing.

Shifting the focus of SLAs

All SLAs should begin with a foundation of operational metrics such as availability and response time. But the service organization must also consider SLAs in such a way as to

Machine-Measured	User-Perception Measurements
Reliability	Responsiveness
Response rates	Communication
Accessibilty	Competency
Security metrics	Credibility
Cost	Courtesy
Other machine-related measures	Business value
	Other business-related intangibles

Table 6.3 Best-practice measures to include in SLAs

accurately track the business value being delivered for each Service Request. For example, there is substantially greater impact when the service organization reports to the company that by delivering 99% network up-time to the sales division, an additional $2 million in revenue was made possible. Reporting simply that the network had 99% availability does not sufficiently demonstrate the true value being provided to the enterprise.

Typical SLAs must be re-examined and changed to reflect that kind of value for each service being provided. For this to happen, the service organization must put in place mechanisms to evaluate and record the metrics that demonstrate business value to the organization. A service organization that provides not only core metrics, but can also put in place a measure of ongoing process improvement, will enhance its perception within the company (see Table 6.3).

Through the process of tying the strategic goals of individual business units with service-team SLAs, an atmosphere of collaboration and cooperation is born. The service group and the Business Unit are 'on the same page' and therefore more likely to work together toward even more innovative solutions.

■ 6.4 Step 4: Start pricing and charge-backs

Consumers who receive goods or services for free often perceive the value as commensurate with what they pay. This holds true for IT Service delivery as well – when the employee customer pays nothing for a service, service delivery becomes an all-you-can-eat buffet. Worse yet, without an established price, the customer's perception may be that internal services come without cost to the organization.

Unfortunately, many service organizations perpetuate this problem through a fixed-price cost allocation model that hides the cost of each service from the consumers of those services. The employee customer treats services as an entitlement, meaning the demand for services can be virtually unconstrained. This puts the service delivery team in the untenable position of needing to allocate scarce resources and rationing services. This inevitably places a strain on the service organization and reinforces the customer's perception of poor customer service.

■ **Path-to-success recommendation:**

When service organizations charge for the services they deliver, the challenge of managing budgets shifts to the employee customer who wants the service. If the price for the service exceeds the benefit, it is the employee customer – not the service team – who makes the business decision.

By implementing a flexible service-based pricing model, the services group can respond to varying levels of demand for services or unexpected projects. This is why the advanced service organization sets a competitive price and charges for the services it delivers.

Price versus costs – two different concepts

There is a very important distinction between the price and the cost of a service:

- **The price** is determined by a combination of the business value the customer places on each service and the amount the customer is willing to pay for a given service.
- **The cost** reflects the actual cost of delivering a service at the customer's expected service level. If your costs for a particular service are higher than the prevailing market price, consider strategic outsourcing as a way to improve the value delivered to employee customers (see "Step 5: Strategic Outsourcing").

Setting competitive pricing

The first step to developing a successful pricing structure is to understand the actual cost of delivering a service. A service organization that runs like a business must continually examine its true costs to perform each service, including labor, materials and overhead. Modern service delivery management applications can help capture the key metrics required to identify actual costs.

■ **Requirements checklist:**

❑ Charge for the services delivered
❑ Set price points by understanding the customer's key business drivers and ensure pricing aligns with the value delivered

In parallel, the service organization should refer to a variety of sources to understand the market rate for each service. There are several sources of information on market prices:

- Industry analyst firms, such as Gartner Group or Forrester Research, talk with hundreds of customers a year about their pricing metrics. These firms offer a range of consulting services to help organizations understand how their service pricing compares to market rates.
- Industry benchmarking consortiums, such as the American Productivity & Quality Center (APQC) or the Shared Services Benchmarking Association, provide a number of alternatives for finding the appropriate price comparisons.
- Responses to RFPs and RFIs from established outsourcing organizations can help you identify the market rate for specific service offerings. Keep in mind that outsourcer prices vary depending on the size of the overall commitment and contract size. Quotes for

providing just two or three services will be much higher than quotes for individual services as part of a comprehensive outsourcing contract.
- Finally, as the managed service marketplace matures, external service providers are increasingly publishing their price lists, which are available most typically on their websites.

By looking at multiple sources, the service group gains insight not only into what others are paying for the services it provides, but also whether it is cost-effective for the service group to be delivering the service internally at all.

As in a stand-alone business, there can be rational reasons to price a service above, at, or below cost. Ideally, a service team is able to price its overall services portfolio above its costs but below the price charged by external providers. This allows the service organization to capture some 'profit' that it can use to invest in creating new service offerings, in finding ways to achieve even greater efficiencies, and in supporting ongoing service team training.

Some services may be cash cows, while others are loss-leaders. The important thing is to make sure that pricing is set in a way that recognizes the difference.

Timing is everything

When the service organization begins to institute a pricing structure for internal customers, there is likely to be substantial resistance within the company. Business Unit customers worry that implementation of a pricing scheme will affect their own bottom line. "We never paid for this before. Why should we begin paying you now?" is a common objection as pricing metrics begin to be published.

At the heart of this concern is often a lack of understanding about the tangible and intangible benefits associated with each service. To counteract this, the leadership and service delivery team members should have tools to evangelize its value proposition at every level of the company.

One of the first steps to establishing the value of each service is to ask the employee customers what each service is worth to them as it is delivered. This can be a formal or informal process – and as simple as asking "What would it cost you if we did not perform this service?" or "What benefit does this service provide you?" This information can be used as a foundation for establishing the value proposition back to the employee customer.

A next step is for the service organization to be proactive in educating the customer about the rationale behind instituting a pricing and charge-back mechanism. The service organization must take adequate time to justify the model and secure support throughout the enterprise. One way of doing this is to announce a timetable under which the policy is to be gradually rolled out, while, at the same time, conducting an outreach program within the company to garner feedback.

> ■ **Requirements checklist:**
> ❑ Let the employee customers help establish the value of services and use that information to justify the charge-backs
> ❑ Before implementing a complete charge-back system, give the business units time to become familiar with the concept that there is a cost to service by publishing a price in the catalog of services

Service organizations that simply begin charging internal customers without properly preparing them for the shift usually encounter stiff resistance. If the Business Units are not given sufficient time to incorporate the expenses into their budget planning process, there will be no funding available to accommodate the service organization.

In the end, the creation of a pricing and charge-back system is vital for the long-term survival of the service organization. For the company at large, the creation of such a system spawns a greater appreciation for the value the service organization adds to the enterprise. While it requires a substantial psychological change for both the service provider and the customer, the potential benefits outweigh the complications.

■ 6.5 Step 5: Evaluate strategic (selective) outsourcing

On average, 10% of IT budgets are spent on outsourced service providers – and the total spent on outsourcing grew faster than any other IT spend category, at 22% from 2001 to 2004.

For many types of services, outsourcers can provide a cost-effective alternative to internal service delivery. But repeated studies show that wholesale outsourcing of complete business processes often delivers less than expected results (see figure 6.3). For instance:
• According to Forrester Research, only 38% of full IT outsourcing agreements are considered a success by the customers;
• According to Dunn & Bradstreet, 50% of outsourcing contracts fail within five years.

Implement an ongoing process to compare internal Service Delivery with outsourced alternatives on a task-by-task basis

At the core of shifting toward operating services like a business is the philosophy of seeking the best provider for every service. This can mean that services that were traditionally provided by internal service groups actually should be sourced to an outside vendor.

While there is an underlying psychology of competition between the service group and outsourcers who threaten to take their place, the internal service delivery chain must have the willingness to look to outside vendors to help in the process of reducing cost and improving service delivery. Once the service organization embraces the notion that an outsourced solution may be operationally and financially beneficial, it can address the notion of the circumstances under which the enterprise should leverage external service providers.

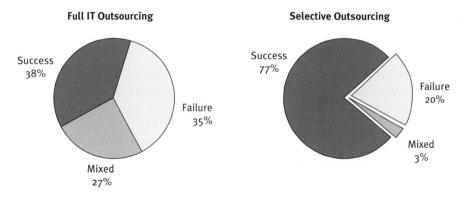

Figure 6.3 Selective outsourcing more successful than full outsourcing

When to outsource

Strategic outsourcing is defined as finding and acquiring the optimal staff resources to execute service delivery, while determining the right mix of outside service providers to maximize the overall value of the service portfolio. The service organization must be willing to recognize areas in which its own offerings do not adequately meet the needs of the customer and take appropriate action to seek a better solution.

■ Path-to-success recommendation:

As the service organization evaluates its overall effectiveness, it should concentrate on identifying services that it cannot deliver on par with similar offerings in the marketplace.

There are instances in which an outside vendor has specific expertise that exceeds that of the organization, or it can provide the service less expensively than can be done internally. Therefore, any service that is particularly time-consuming or costly to deliver internally is an ideal candidate for outsourcing.

The principal manner in which an internal service organization determines the need for external providers is by a thorough, honest and realistic assessment of its core competencies. To do this, the organization must first have an understanding of how much it costs to deliver the services it offers, the service levels it achieves, and metrics on quality.

The problem is that many internal service organizations do not maintain a detailed record of their own operations and costs. They are, therefore, ill-prepared to do any meaningful comparisons. Fortunately, modern Service Catalog and Delivery Management systems automatically capture the data required to resolve this problem as an integral part of the ordering and delivery of services.

Internal service delivery organizations need to consider the fact that external service providers frequently back-load cost recovery over a multi-year period. The organization must take this into account when evaluating the relative cost of the outsourced solution. It may appear that the outsourcer's pricing for the first year is substantially more attractive than keeping a function in-house. However, over the complete term of the relationship, the outsourced option may in fact prove to be more costly.

By implementing this process of careful self-evaluation, the organization can identify the service functions that are best kept inside the company. The internal service group must selectively determine the services it provides - and which should be outsourced - based on a detailed understanding of its own competencies and shortfalls. It then can begin the search for external service providers that offer the best opportunity for the organization to reduce the overall cost of doing business while maintaining high service quality.

■ Requirements checklist:

❑ Avoid the temptation to outsource broken service processes (which simply exports the problem to the outsourcer, thereby increasing the likelihood that the outsourcer will fail as well)

❑ Integrate the external service provider into the service delivery team so the employee customer is indifferent as to who provides services

The external service provider should be fully integrated into the service chain in such a way as to be completely invisible to the customer. A customer who orders a service, such as re-wiring the electrical lines in an office, does not care whether the electrician who performs the job is internal or external. They simply want the office re-wired as inexpensively and efficiently as possible.

Invest in outsourcer relationships like a partnership

Strategic outsourcing is a partnering relationship where both parties should do everything possible to ensure mutual success. The success of the external service provider and internal service team are inextricably linked. As a result, any interaction between the two parties, from initial contract negotiation to subsequent arbitration, should focus on achieving common goals with well-defined cost and performance objectives.

Since strategic relationships require escalation, dispute resolution and compromise, it's vitally important to implement clear lines of communication between the internal service group and the outsourcer. This means that vendor contracts and SLAs must include clear metrics to track performance and costs - with an agreed-to mechanism for monitoring compliance and communicating issues on a frequent and ongoing basis.

This partnership requires a collaborative working relationship between the internal service team and its outsourcing partners. External service providers that are treated fairly by the organization are far more likely to be flexible in the face of a continuously changing business landscape. If leadership within the internal service organization consistently makes unreasonable demands of the external service provider, it will breed contentiousness and resentment that ultimately damages the relationship and its chances for success.

■ 6.6 Step 6: Report, monitor and refine

It is critical for the service organization to continually improve upon the processes it has in place. This is in order to remain competitive with outside vendors as well as to enhance the service organization's productivity, ensure cost containment and improve service levels. The service team must leverage process improvement and formal measurement programs to maximize its reliability, effectiveness and efficiency.

Unfortunately, many organizations do not measure the operational effectiveness of their internal service functions. Because of this, there is no mechanism in place to provide accurate reporting of performance, and the organization is left without the ability to make positive adjustments to the operational structure.

Companies that begin to run services like a business find that with new Service Catalog and Delivery Management systems, key service delivery and customer satisfaction metrics are captured automatically. Every transaction is logged and tracked on a step-by-step basis because of the very nature of an automated ordering and fulfillment process. This helps to benchmark services and quantify service delivery team staffing because the time it takes to complete each task is captured. By reviewing the frequency of demand for a given service and the time it takes to fulfill each order, the organization is able to constantly refine its operation to deliver the best possible level of service to its customers.

There are four constituencies that should be provided with frequent reports on the performance of the service organization:
- **Internal customer:** This is the principal audience for the service group because it is their feedback that allows the group to gain visibility into customer satisfaction. The customer base should receive information regularly that validates the business value it receives from the service organization.
- **Service group:** The service group itself should use regular performance reporting to identify shortfalls and implement remedies, such as engaging an outside vendor, in order to deliver quality services at a lower cost.
- **Senior management:** The executives who oversee and govern the internal service organization's service delivery must be provided with very high-level reports on costs and performance in order to make well-informed budgetary decisions.
- **External Service Providers:** ESPs and outsourcers that are incorporated into the service chain need to receive performance reports about their effectiveness as part of the organization's overall service offering.

Metrics alone provide little to no value

To use performance metrics effectively, company management must focus on how data is implemented, reported and acted upon. Metrics must be relevant, practical, actionable, reported and owned. Relevance means that the metrics must be directly tied to a specific goal or objective for the success of a given function. It also is important to keep the metrics as simple as possible and resist the urge to measure too many data points.

> ### ■ Path-to-success recommendation:
> If the organization monitors more than five key performance metrics for a given service, at best the impact of the information provided is severely depleted or, at worst, the data is so overwhelming as to be totally useless.

The data then must be actionable, enabling changes in practice or behavior that lead to an improvement in these metrics. Lastly, there must be an individual who is held accountable for each of the metrics being analyzed. Without the element of ownership, there is no way to ensure that steps will be taken on a regular basis to enhance operational performance and efficiency.

Measurement and quality control are critical to the continued success of the service group. The service organization should institutionalize continuous process improvement - leveraging competitive data, benchmarking information and internal performance metrics that are regularly collected, analyzed and acted upon. To do so, it must put in place mechanisms for continuous measurement and reporting of key performance indicators that educate senior management about which service operations can be streamlined.

Gartner points out that the concept of process improvement originated in the manufacturing arena, where studies have shown that manufacturing workers tend to be twice as productive as service workers. This is because continuous process improvement is incorporated in the advanced manufacturing organization. These same practices can be implemented for internal service organizations. Over time, process improvements improve the service organization's ability to control the service levels and pricing structure for its internal customers.

■ 6.7 Putting it all together: transforming the IT Organization

Massive organizational transformation, as described in these past few pages, can prove to be difficult. Altering the beliefs, habits, roles and responsibilities of so many people engaged in such a wide variety of activities across the enterprise can appear, at the outset, to be an impossible task. But when undertaken with care and planning, the results are overwhelmingly positive. Companies that have accepted the challenge and implemented these strategies are realizing enhanced operational efficiency and greater customer satisfaction.

7

Guide To Supplemental Materials

The CD included with this book contains examples of worksheets, templates, and project plans which can be used to accelerate the development of a Service Catalog project. These documents are intended to be used as-is or modified to address the unique needs of each organization. Each file is available in pdf format. This file can be opened in Adobe Acrobat. In addition we have also added a MS Project file on the cd-rom. This file can only be used when MS Project (Version 2000 and upwards) is available on your system.

Resource Name (File Name)	Description
Invitation to join ServiceCatalogs.com (ServiceCatalogs Invitation.pdf)	Invitation and link to participate in a growing community of IT professionals working on Service Catalog initiatives, who share with each other their resources and experiences
Service Offering Template (Service Offering Template.pdf)	Template for documenting a Service Offering, with a focus on the business customer as the key stakeholder
Service Specification Sheet (Service Specification Sheet.pdf)	Questionnaire to guide the definition and documentation of an IT Service
Generic System Specification Form (Generic System Specification Form.pdf)	Template for documenting an IT System and its related components
Service Request Business Requirements Questionnaire (Service Request Business Requirements Questionnaire.pdf)	Questionnaire to guide the definition, documentation and development of Service Request processes
Sample Service Level Management Project Charter (SLM - Project Charter.pdf)	Starting point for developing a SLM project charter
Sample Service Level Management Project Plan (SLM – Project Plan Template.mpp, MS Project file)	Starting point for developing a SLM project plan
Sample Service Level Agreement 1 (SLM - SLA Example.pdf)	Sample SLA document, which can be used to provide detail related to the delivery of Service Offerings, IT Services and/or IT Systems

Sample Service Level Agreement 2 (SLM - SLA Example 2.pdf)	Sample SLA document, which can be used to provide detail related to the delivery of Service Offerings, IT Services and/or IT Systems
Operating Level Agreement Template (OLA Template.pdf)	Template for documenting an Operating Level Agreement
Sample Operating Level Agreement (OLA Sample.pdf)	Sample OLA document, which can be used to provide detail related to the delivery of an SLA